PAST & PRESENT

WOODWARD

Opposite: This undated photograph is of the City Bakery in the 600 block of Main Street, owned and operated by Louis B. Geismar (far left). The bakery opened in 1894 and remained open until Geismar's death in 1911. After he died, the family left Woodward, except for son Alex, who eventually became executive vice president of the Bank of Woodward. (Courtesy of the Plains Indians & Pioneers Museum.)

PAST & PRESENT

WOODWARD

Dr. Deena K. Fisher and Robin D. Hohweiler

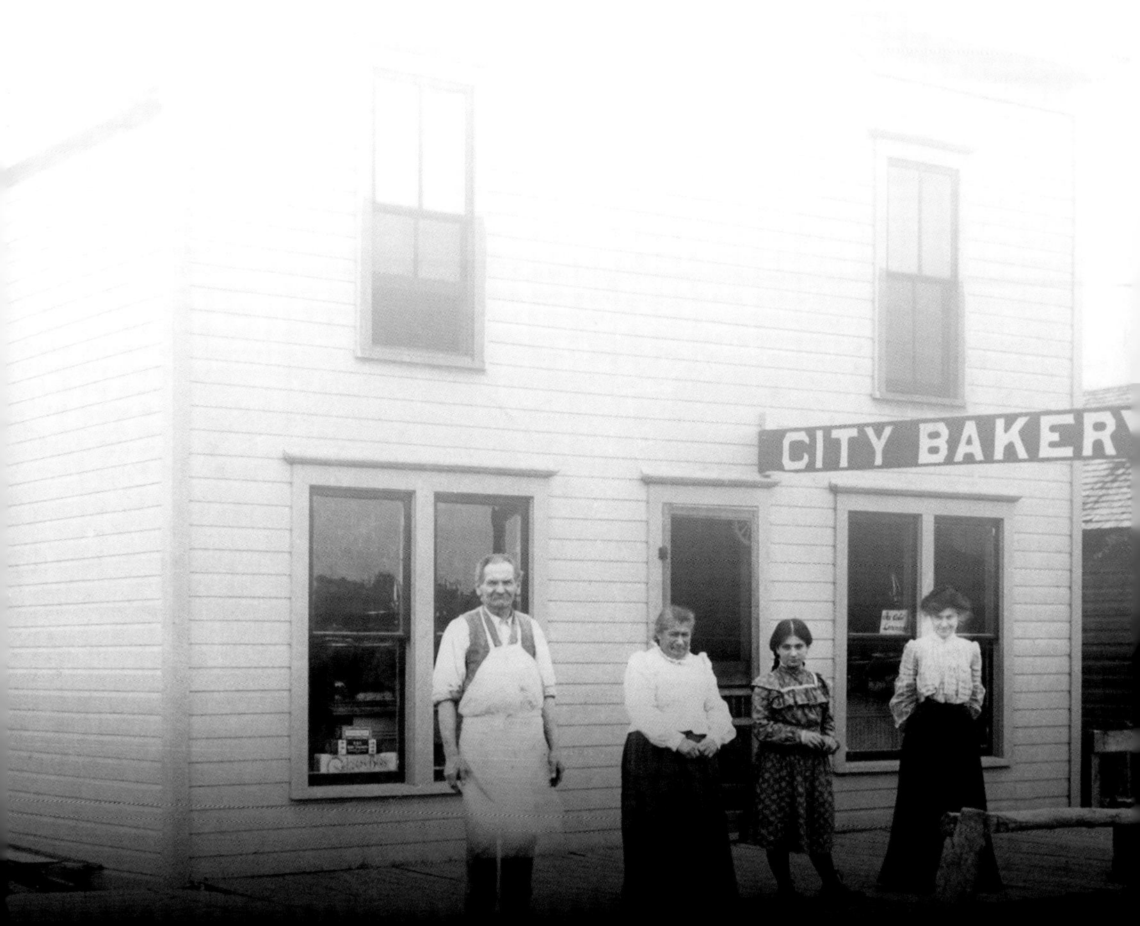

ISBN 978-1-4671-0597-2

Library of Congress Control Number: 2020945059

Published by Arcadia Publishing
Charleston, South Carolina

Printed in the United States of America

For all general information, please contact Arcadia Publishing:
Telephone 843-853-2070
Fax 843-853-0044
E-mail sales@arcadiapublishing.com
For customer service and orders:
Toll-Free 1-888-313-2665

Visit us on the Internet at www.arcadiapublishing.com

Front Cover: The Stine-Bradbury House was originally built by banker Len Stine in 1916 on the corner of Tenth Street and Kansas Avenue. The home was also occupied by the Harold Bradbury family, who made some significant modern improvements to the home. This iconic Woodward mansion has stood the test of time despite suffering minor roof damage during the 1947 Woodward tornado. (Past image courtesy of the Plains Indians & Pioneers Museum; present image by Robin Hohweiler.)

Back Cover: This photograph, probably from the late 1940s or early 1950s, shows four cowboys seated on the ground during a performance of the Woodward Elks Rodeo. The Woodward Elks Rodeo, an annual event for more than 90 years, got its start in 1929 when cattlemen who were members of the Woodward Elks Lodge set out to sponsor a rodeo for the benefit of the local community. (Courtesy of the Plains Indians & Pioneers Museum.)

Contents

Acknowledgments

First and foremost, the authors wish to thank the museum board and staff of the Plains Indians & Pioneers Museum in Woodward, Oklahoma, for allowing access to their vast collection of photographic images from Woodward's past. Without that access, there would not be a *Woodward* Past & Present book. Unless otherwise noted, all the past images in this publication are from the museum's collection and all present images were made by Robin Hohweiler.

Of the museum staff, thanks to Robert Roberson, executive director; Tammy Hawbaker, curator; and Nancy McCormick, gift shop manager, in particular for their time and patience in helping us locate images, scan images, exchange documents, and offer advice.

The authors also wish to thank Tom Fisher for his effort in getting photographs of the Woodward elementary schools that were otherwise unavailable. Dean Fisher was instrumental in helping to obtain the past photograph and historical timeline of Saint Peter Catholic Church. Connie Terry, head librarian at Woodward Public Library, provided us a great photograph of the old Carnegie Library that was a second home to so many people years ago. Also, thanks go to Pastor Ronnie Hopkins, who helped locate a photograph and timeline of the First Christian Church.

The authors are, of course, grateful to Woodward Public Schools, Saint Peter Catholic Church, the Woodward Public Library, High Plains Technology Center, and the First Christian Church for allowing the use of whatever photographs and information they provided.

Thank you to Robin Miller, general manager of the Woodward Nitrogen Complex, who bravely (and on very short notice) navigated the necessary corporate channels that allowed us to publish that spectacular photograph of the CF Industries plant west of town.

Thank you to Dr. Tom Lucas and Ron Hohweiler for helping sort out the "mystery" of the actual location of the Armour Creameries (Hint: it isn't where most people think it was).

Finally, it would be remiss not to thank Arcadia Publishing for publishing this book. Also, thanks to Lindsey Givens and Stacia Bannerman for having faith in the idea, patiently answering questions, and providing encouragement along the way.

Thanks to everyone else who contributed information, listened to the idea, and encouraged success. Now, go buy a book!

—Deena K. Fisher and Robin D. Hohweiler

Introduction

Many books have been written about western Oklahoma history, including the city of Woodward. The authors set out to add another testament to the rich, colorful, and unique history of an important commercial center and way of life for northwest Oklahoma in both the territorial and post-statehood days.

Woodward: Past & Present offers a visual record of the repurposing of older buildings for a new age and use by people likely not yet born when the structures were originally built.

Robin Hohweiler was raised in Woodward and attended Woodward Public Schools. His love for the area and its people brought him back home following careers in the US Navy and the US intelligence community. Robin is a published writer and (very) amateur filmmaker who currently works as the director of social media for the Plains Indians & Pioneers Museum. His family has been ranching and farming in northwest Oklahoma for more than 100 years. He and his wife, Mary Ann, and three dogs of indeterminate ancestry live on the family farm just east of Fargo, Oklahoma.

Dr. Deena K. Fisher, a native of Elk City, Oklahoma, has lived and worked in Woodward since 1996 and became the dean and professor of history of the Woodward campus of Northwestern Oklahoma State University in 2002. She has published extensively throughout her academic career. Deena has a deep passion for history and is the current president of the board of directors of the Oklahoma Historical Society. She and her husband, Tom, reside in Woodward with their two dogs, Rowdy and Maverick.

As with any publication, there must be "nuggets"—those bits of information that a reader has never known and transforms mere reading into a joyous and delightful ride through a time that few of us experienced. We have done our utmost to ensure the accuracy of these nuggets, and we certainly hope you will enjoy reading them as much as we enjoyed writing about them.

A quick word about locations. Any publication that deals with structures that no longer exist runs the risk of incorrectly stating the exact location of that structure. We did our very best to avoid those location errors but found that, for reasons unknown, there were shifts in address numbering. We have marked those locations by stating their proximity to the original locations.

We hope you enjoy this book. Happy reading!

CHAPTER 1

COMMERCE

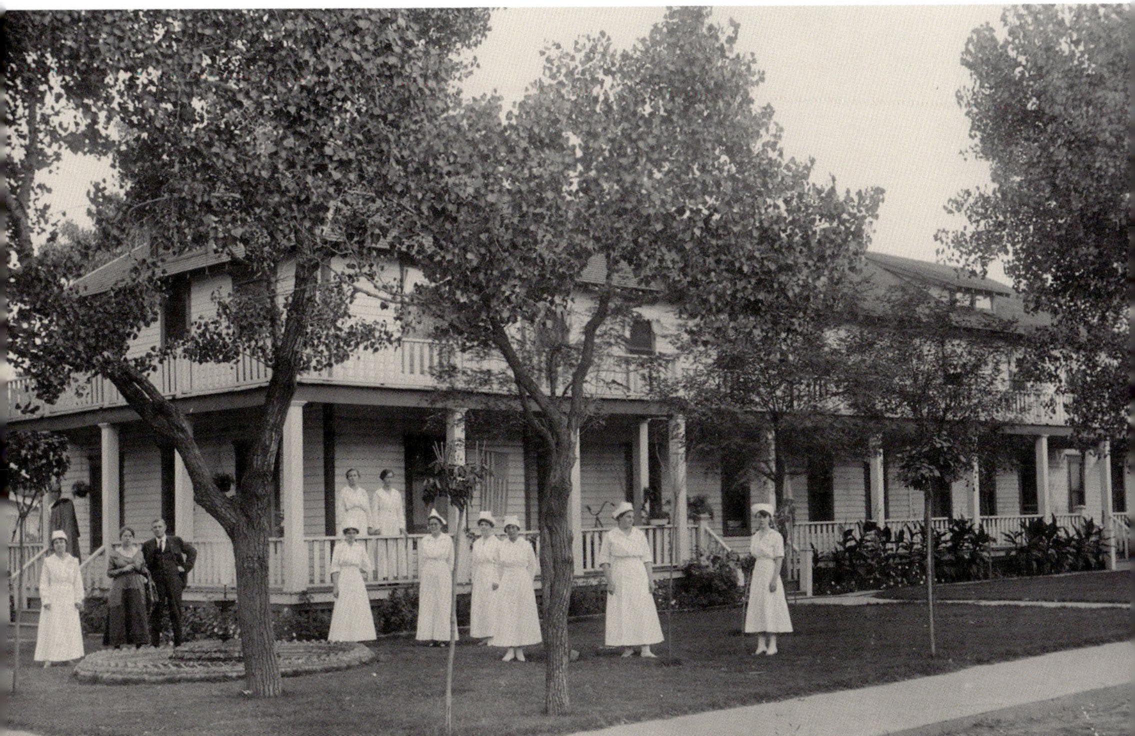

Woodward's first real hospital was on the southeast corner of Texas Avenue and Seventh Street. Started by Dr. G.M. Tracy, the hospital had 15 beds. It was later converted into apartments and was finally razed in the 1980s. The lot remains empty to this day. This photograph dates to 1917.

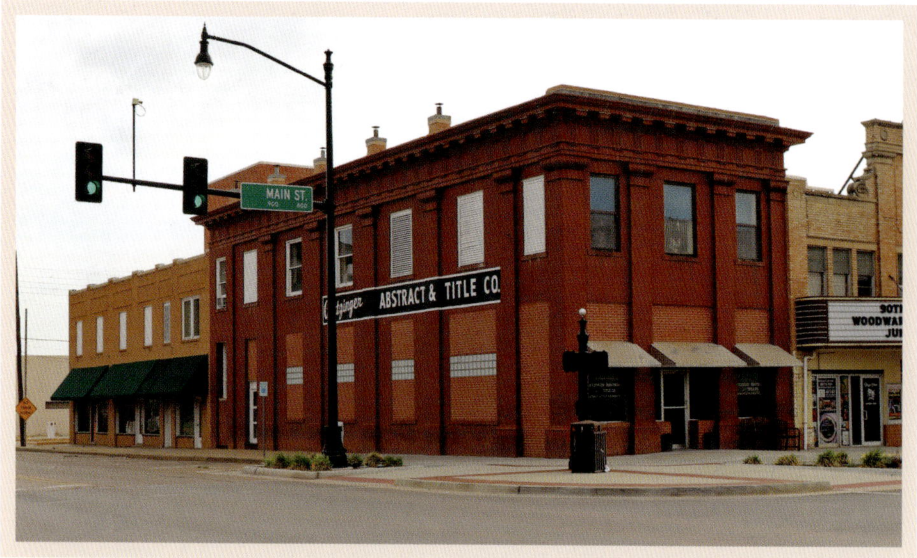

The Gerlach Bank was built in 1905 on the corner of Ninth and Main Streets. The wagons in the vintage photograph are loaded with broom corn, a major cash crop at the time, and are lined up to unload at the O.W. Cox Grain and Feed Co. just across the railroad tracks (northeast of the present-day BNSF Railway depot). The building has served as the home of Goetzinger Abstract & Title Co. since 1933.

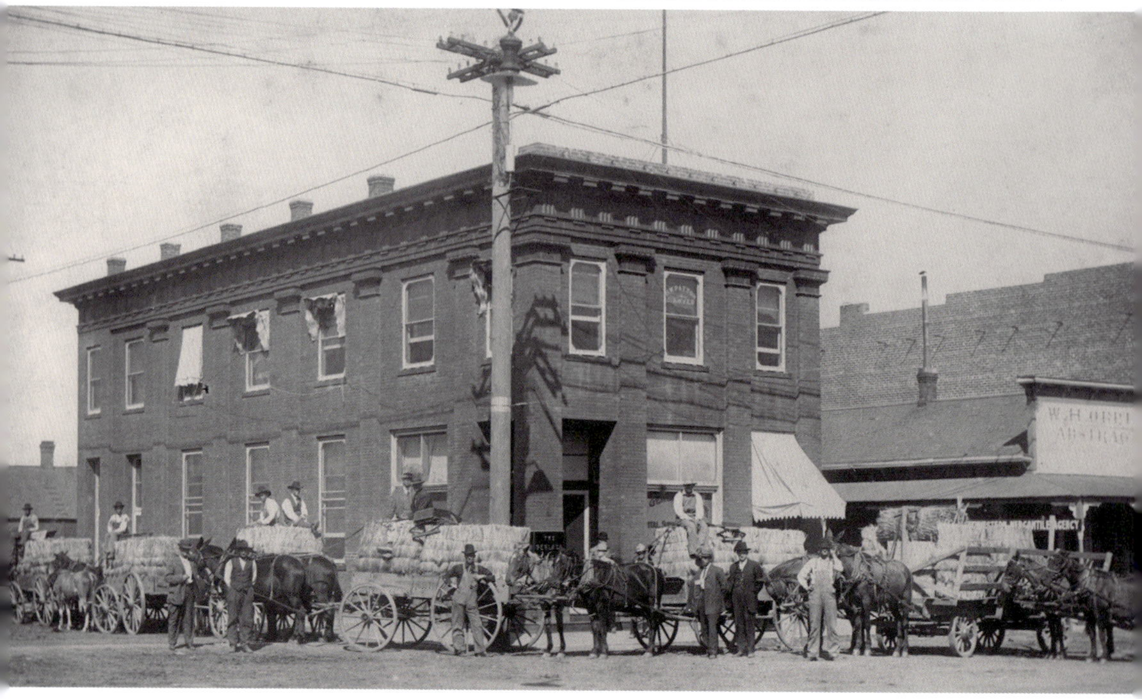

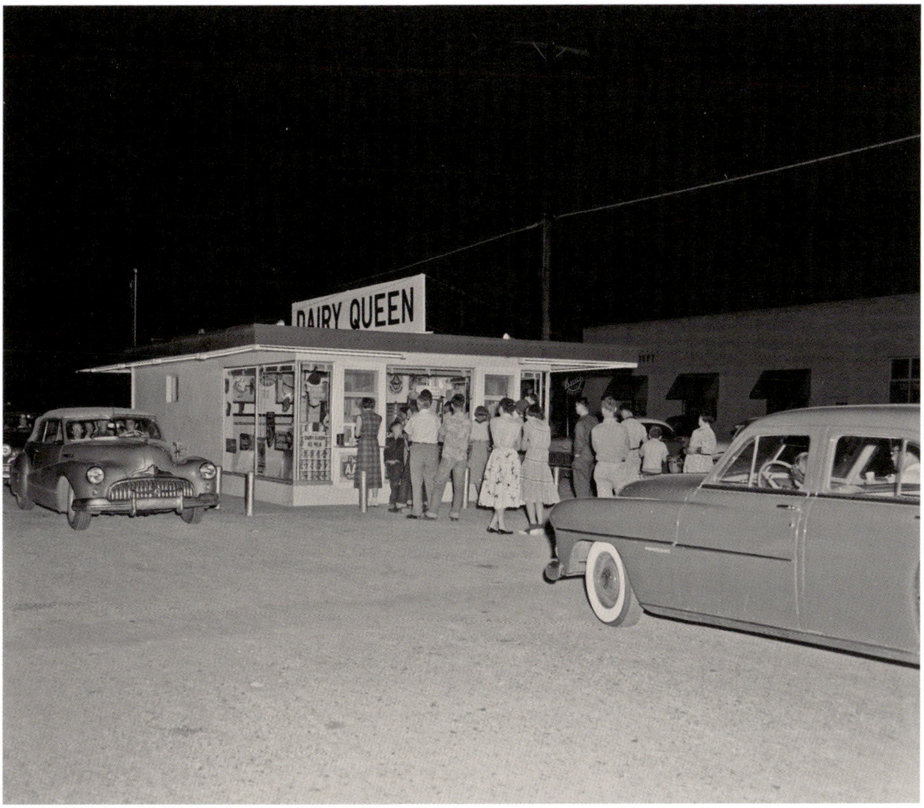

An iconic gathering spot since the early 1950s, the Dairy Queen at 1223 Main Street has served thousands of frozen treats and food to locals. From the Dilly Wagon that crawled city streets in the summer, bringing fresh dairy treats to the kids, to the old fireworks stand (when the city still allowed them to be sold) at the back of the lot, Woodward's DQ has remained at the same location for decades.

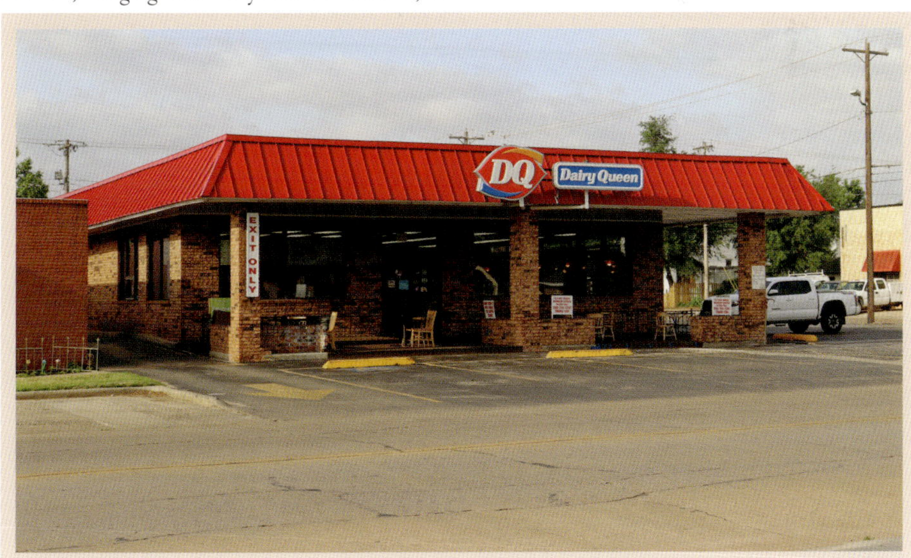

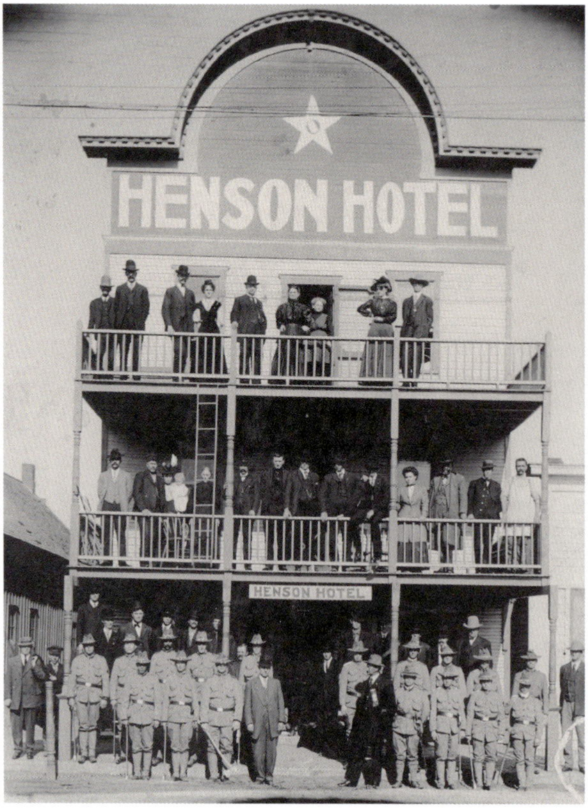

The Henson Hotel was at 512 Main Street, on the north side of the street. The group on the ground wearing what appears to be Spanish-American War–era uniforms are identified as Modern Woodmen of the World (note the axes—nothing says welcome to our hotel like men with axes out front). The hotel operated from 1913 to 1922 and was a multi-story brick structure with a wooden facade. The present location shown approximates the location of the hotel.

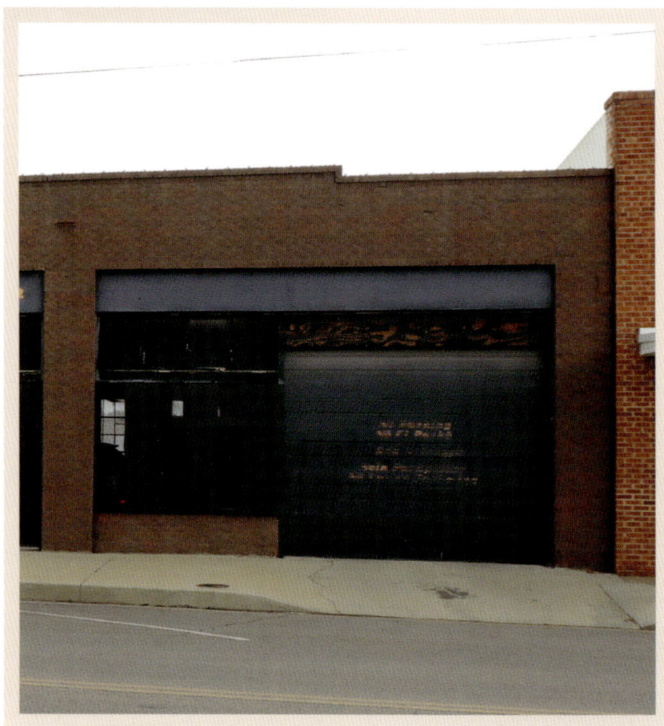

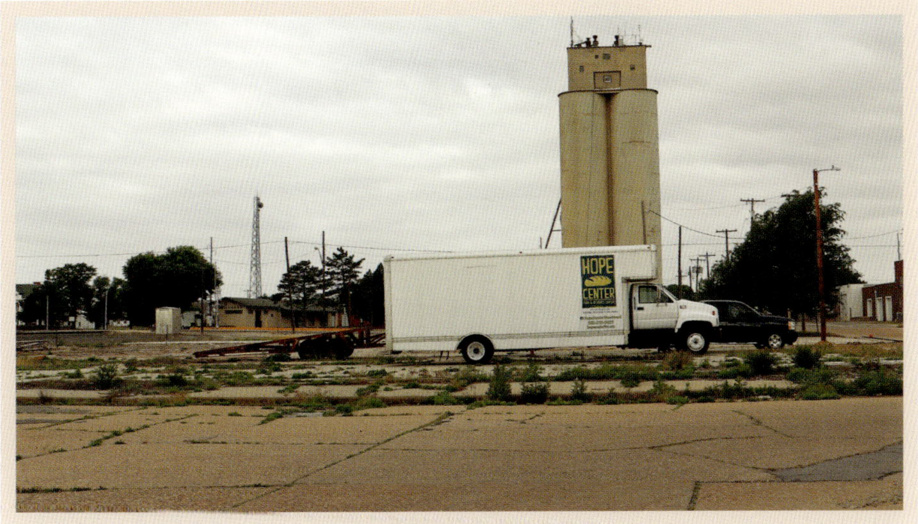

Woodward Steam Laundry was at 901 Eighth Street and was in business long before Statehood in 1907. The name was changed to Woodward Electric Sanitary Laundry and later to Henry Hunter's Dry Cleaners and Laundry in 1927 when it was purchased by Henry Hunter of Elk City, Oklahoma. During the years that it served as Henry Hunter's company, a steam whistle that sounded twice daily at noon and 5:00 p.m. could be heard across the city.

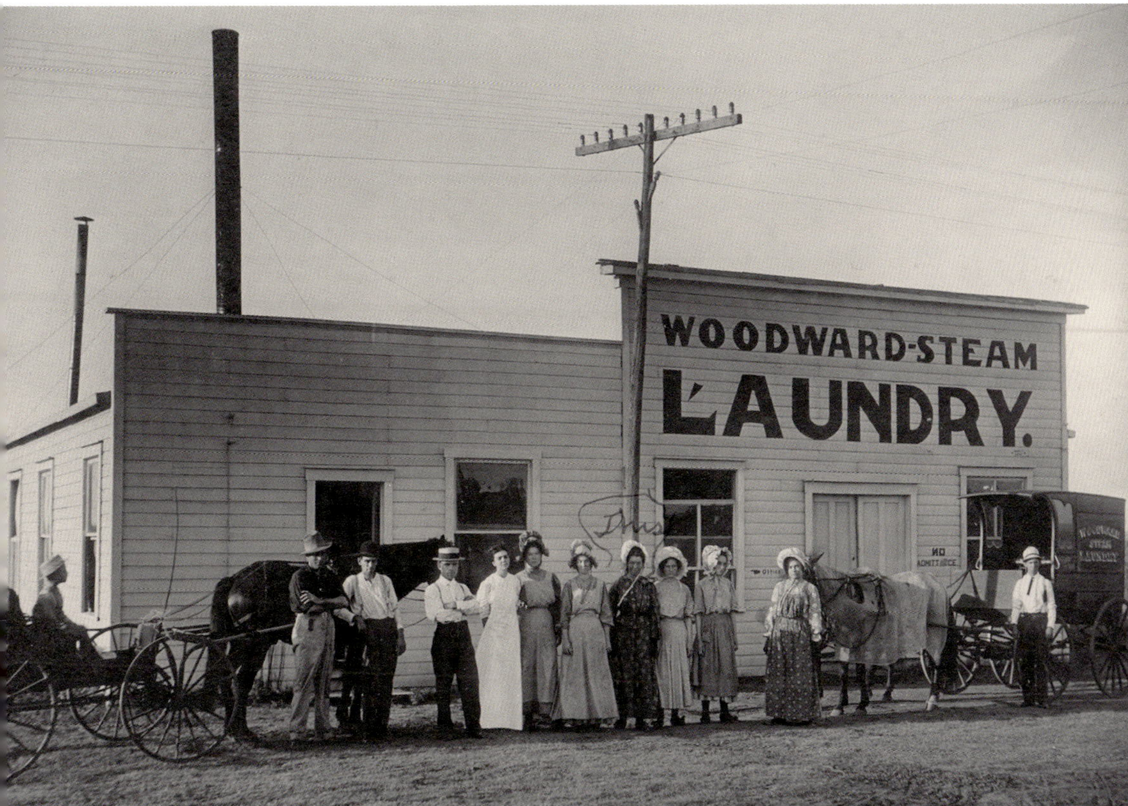

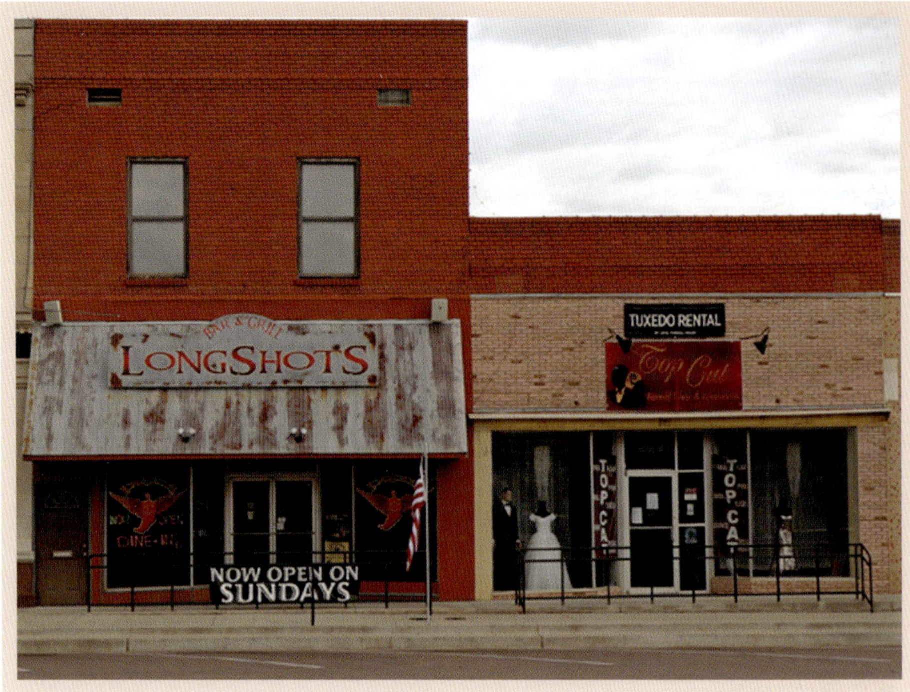

The Martinson General Store was between Eighth and Ninth Streets on the north side of Main Street. Constructed in 1895, the upstairs portion of the building was known as the Opera House and was used for a variety of functions, including recitals, plays, funerals, and even courtroom trials. "Uncle" Dick Woodward moved his saddle shop into the east side of the building in the late 1890s. Today, the location houses Long Shots Bar & Grill and Top Cat Formal Wear & Accessories.

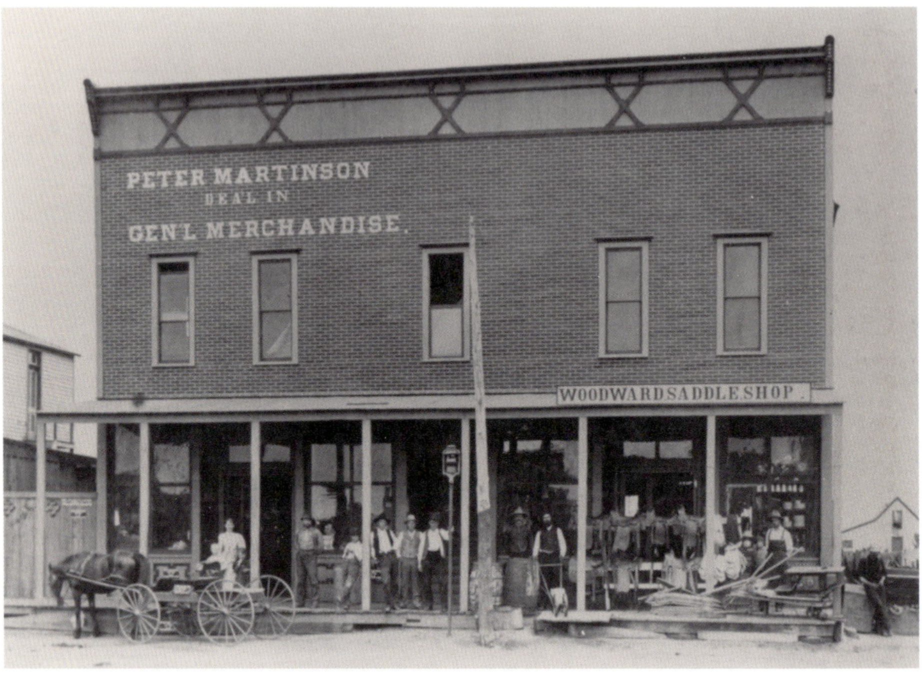

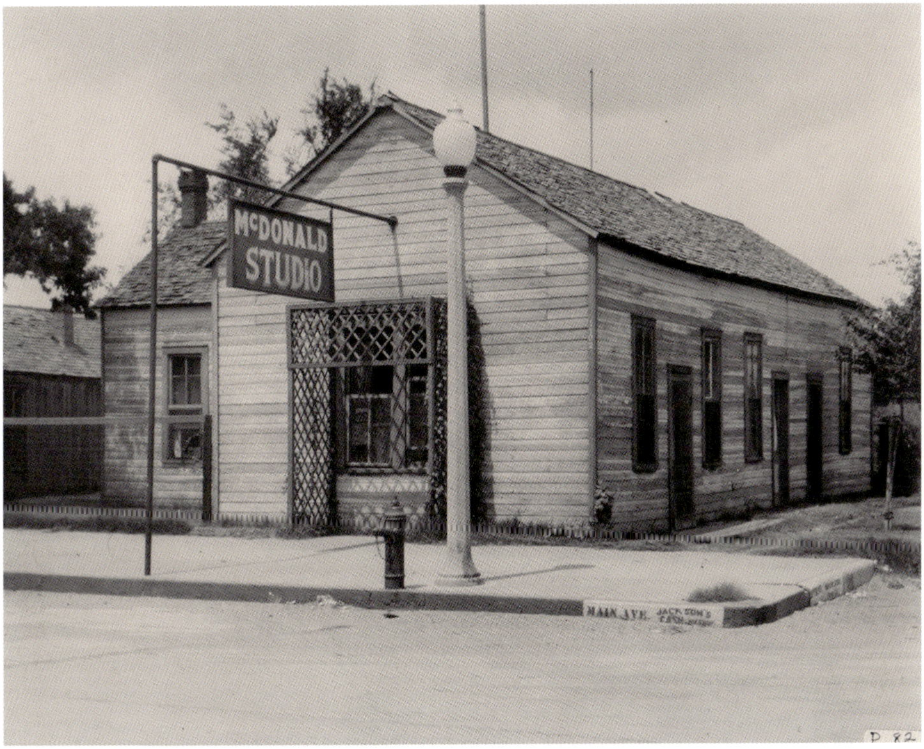

The second McDonald Studio was in a frame building that served as the original federal land office at 11th and Main Streets. The image dates to sometime in the early 1920s. The McDonalds moved the studio a few doors east to 1018 Main Street, where it remained for the rest of the 20th century. The oddly positioned cottage-style building that went up on the lot was used as a service station and today houses the Main Street Woodward offices.

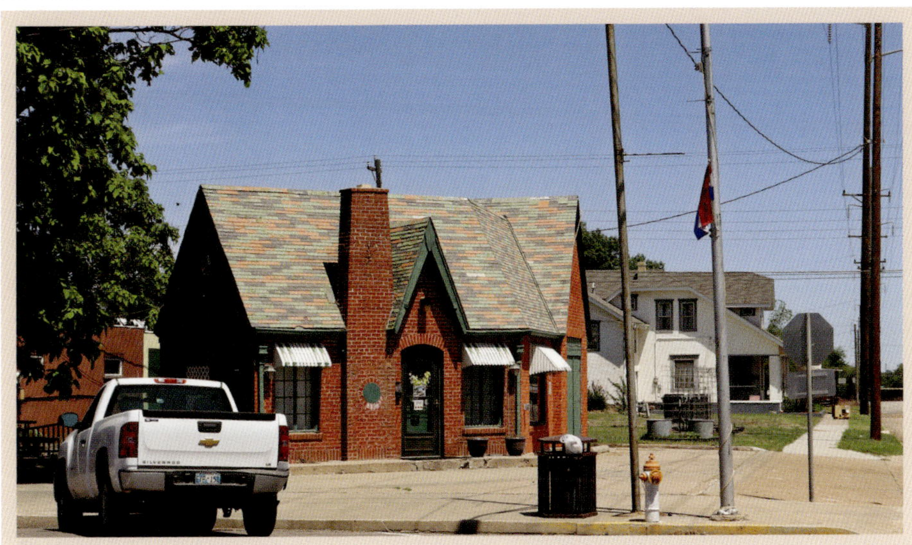

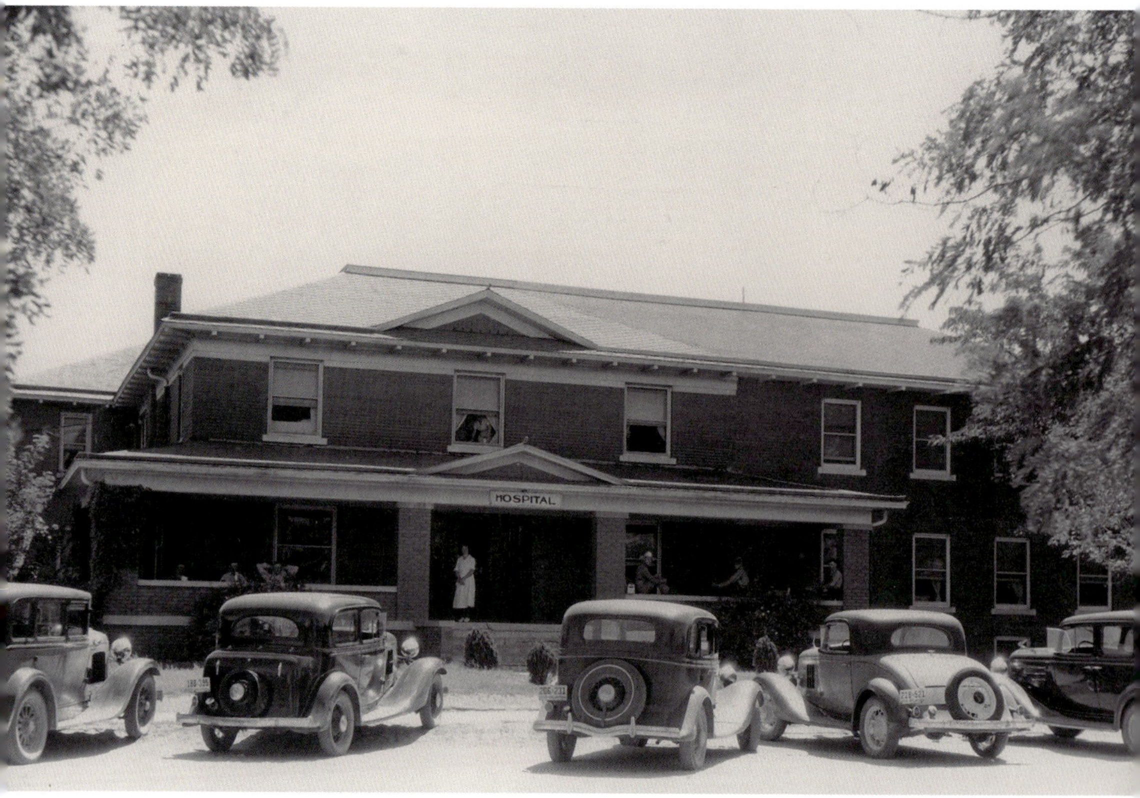

The old Woodward General Hospital at Fourth Street and Locust Avenue opened in 1926 as a premier healthcare facility for Woodward and surrounding communities. The horrific Woodward tornado of 1947 stretched the hospital's ability to serve the community to its limits, with the dead laid out on the lawn in front and the injured lined up in the hallways and in the basement. The building remains but is in a state of disrepair.

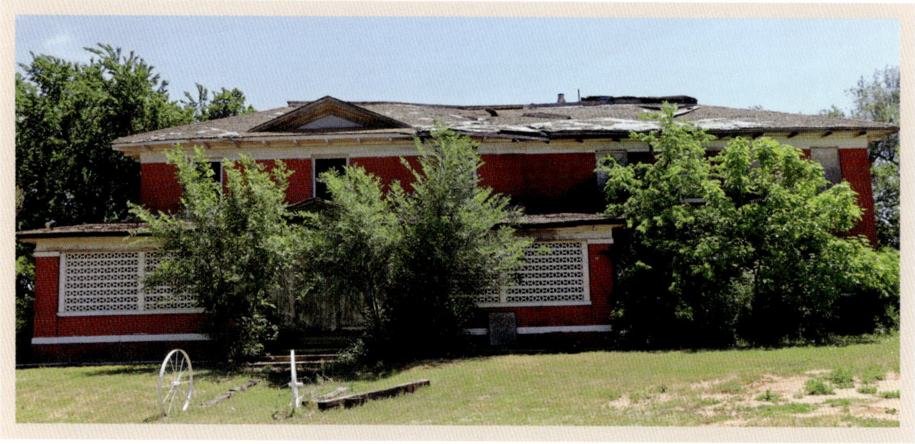

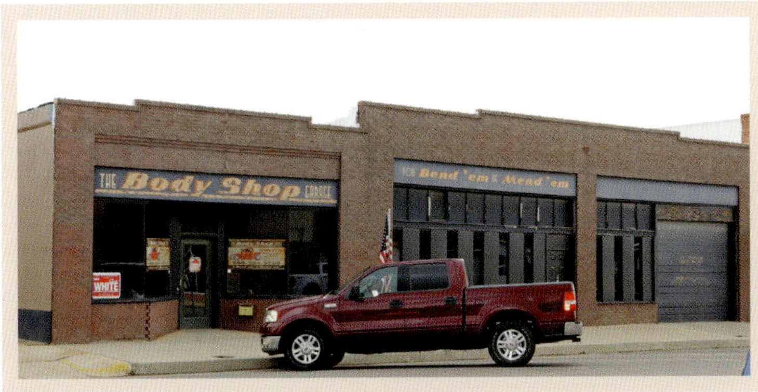

The photograph below shows the Nelson Motor Co. in Woodward at 516 Main Street, with Earl Nelson standing in front in probably December 1946 (note the garland stretched across Main). Besides being the only Jeep and Willys dealer in Woodward, Nelson was a farmer and avid square dancer. He also operated a tire retread operation at the back of the building. The location today houses the Body Shop.

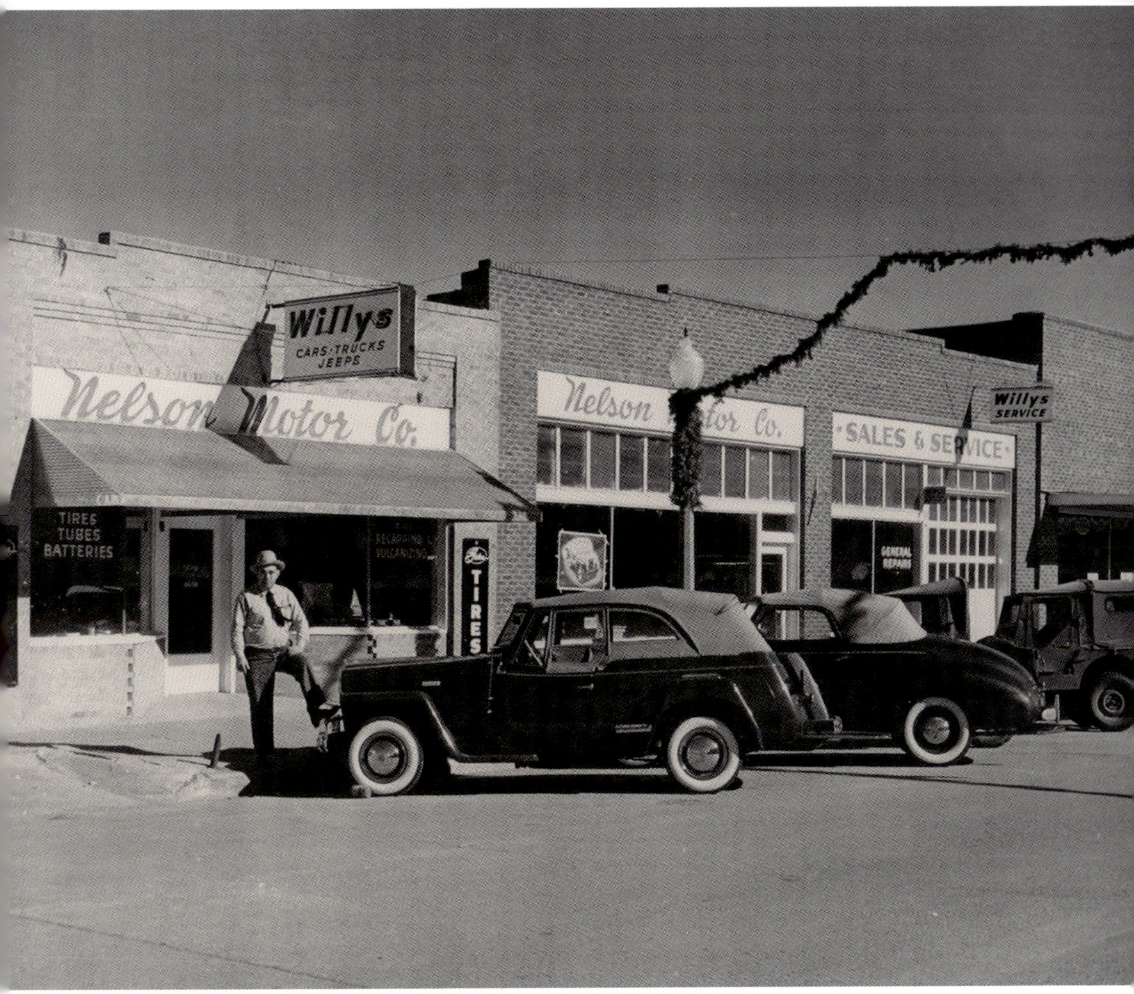

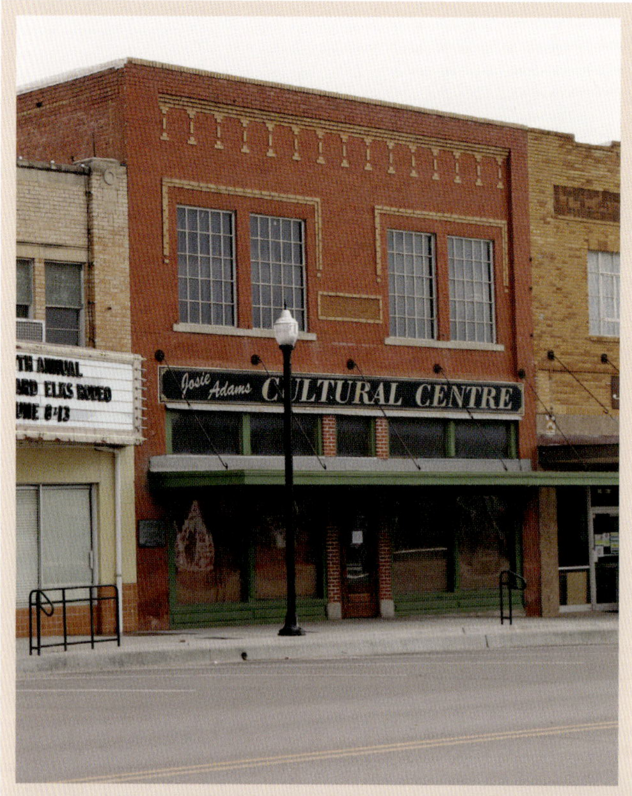

This photograph of Breck's Variety store at 818 Main Street dates to the late 1950s. It later served as a Ben Franklin retail store. The building was originally erected as the Boehm Meat Market in the early 20th century. Today, the same structure houses the Josie Adams Cultural Centre, part of the Woodward Arts and Theatre Council complex. It is used for a variety of purposes, including receptions, meetings, and charity events.

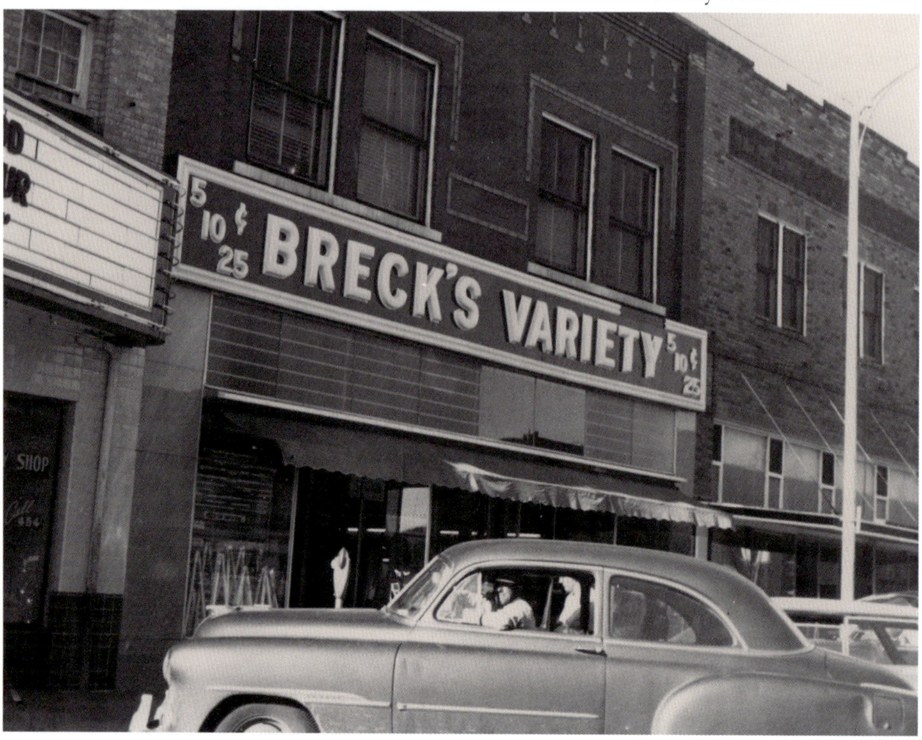

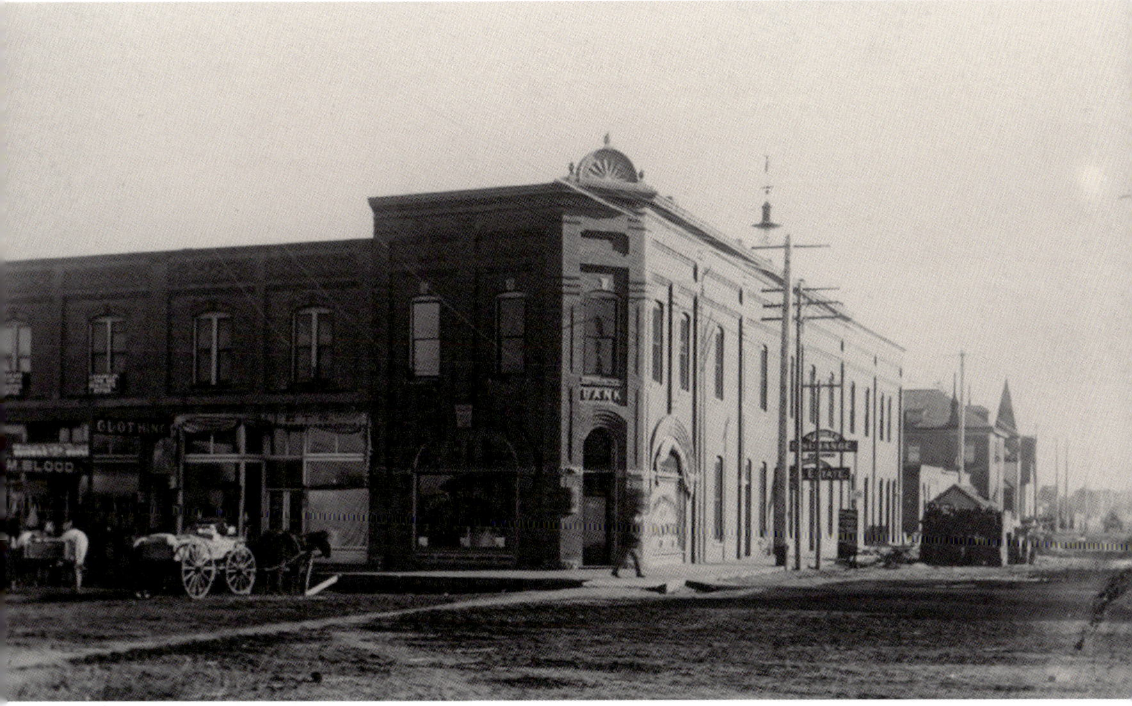

The vintage image shows the First National Bank building (owned by L.L. Stine) on the corner of Eighth and Main Streets in the early 1900s. The image below shows the same building in 2020. After the collapse of First National Bank in 1932, the building most notably served as a shoe store, Hopkins' Shoemart, for much of the 20th and early 21st centuries. Today, it houses the Homestead Decor + Gifts shop.

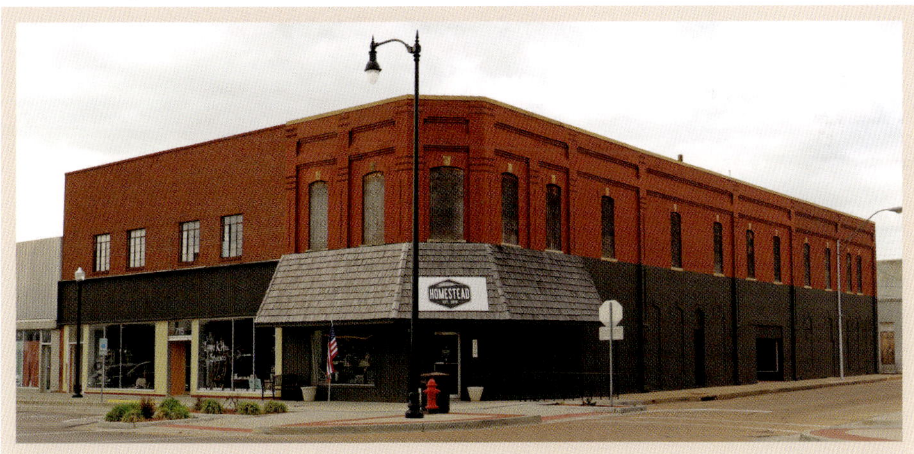

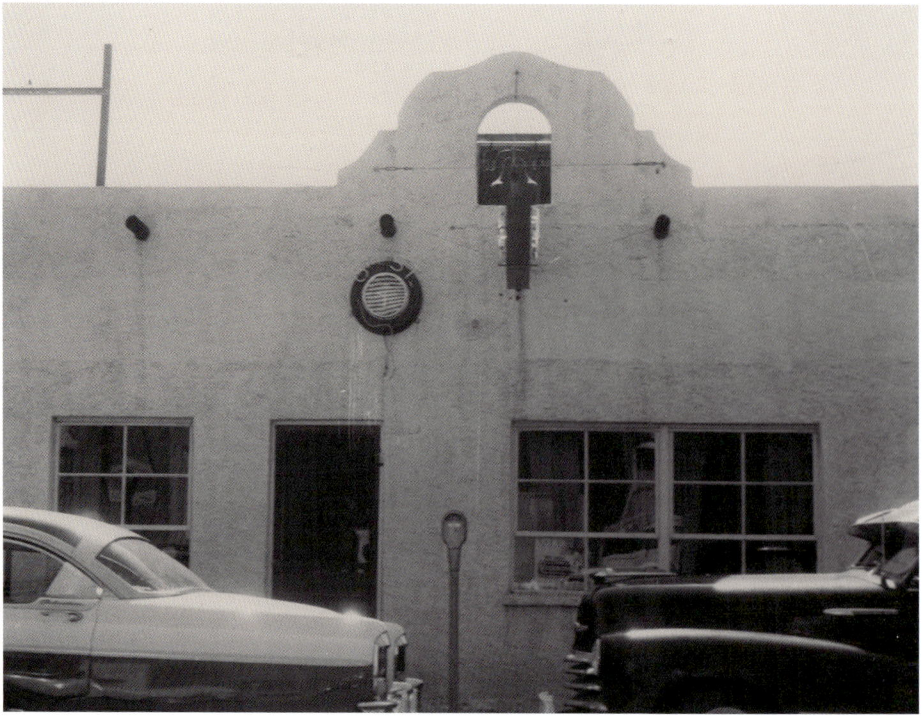

The vintage image shows the Eighth Street Cafe in 1959. Located at 1111 Eighth Street in Woodward, the building, with its Southwest-style architecture, was a restaurant for most of its life. It was a great location when Eighth Street carried the highway leading north out of town. American Legion Post 19 uses the building today. The only real difference in the building is that the main entrance was moved farther down the facade.

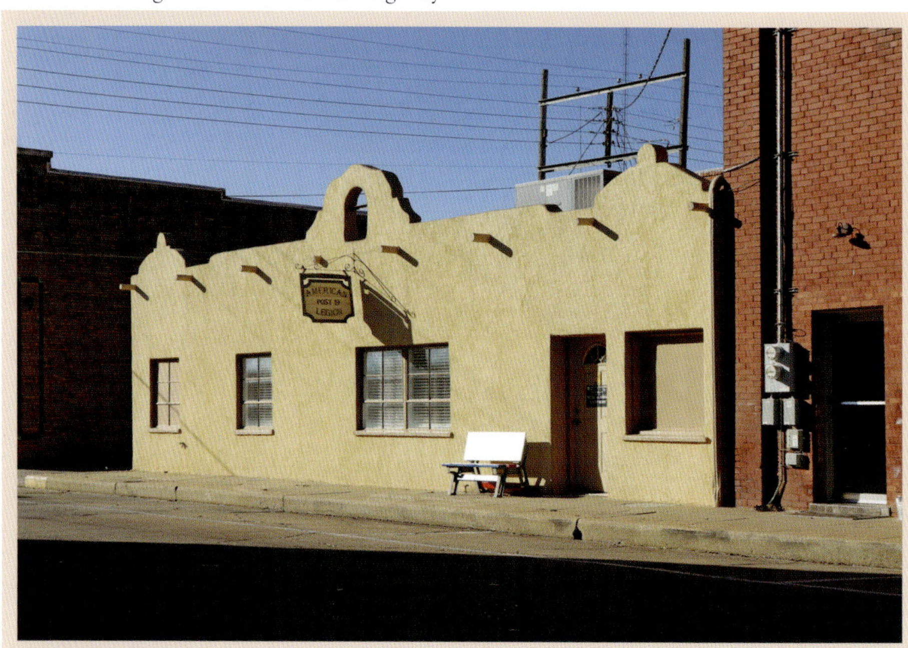

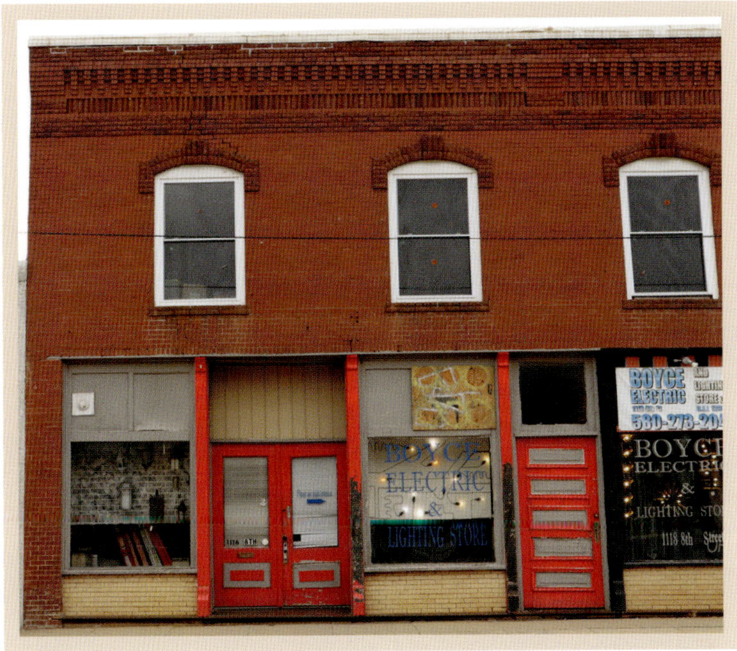

The photograph below dates to 1916 and shows the first-place winner of the 200 Mile Road Race. The finish time was 4 hours, 13 minutes, and 54 seconds. The car is shown parked in front of the Buick dealership on Eighth Street between Main Street and Texas Avenue. The building today serves as the home of Boyce Electric. The fire station in 1916 was just to the left and today houses an upholstery shop.

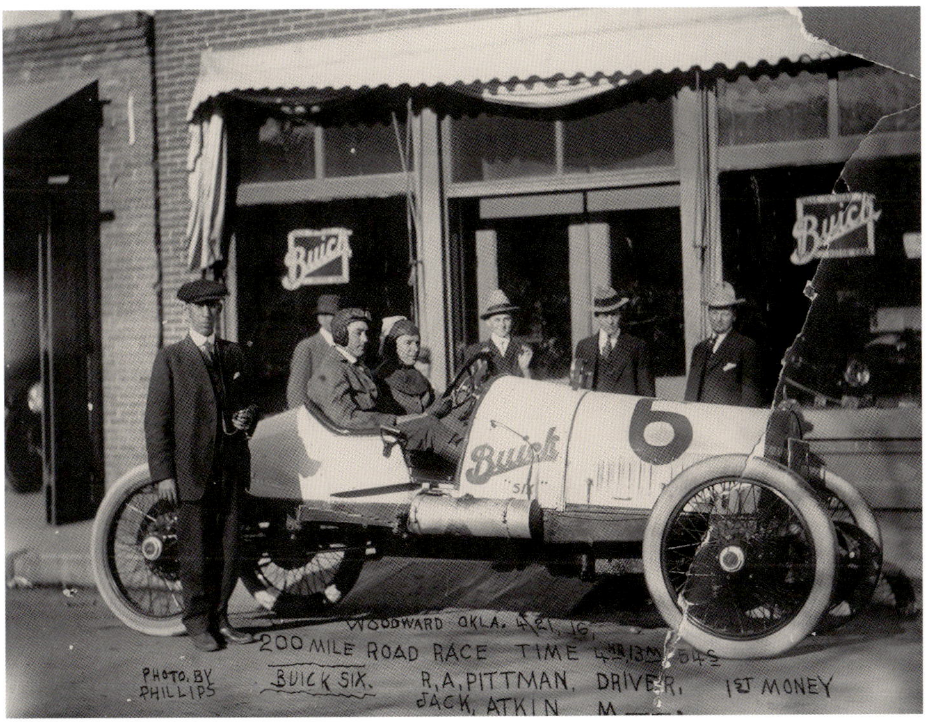

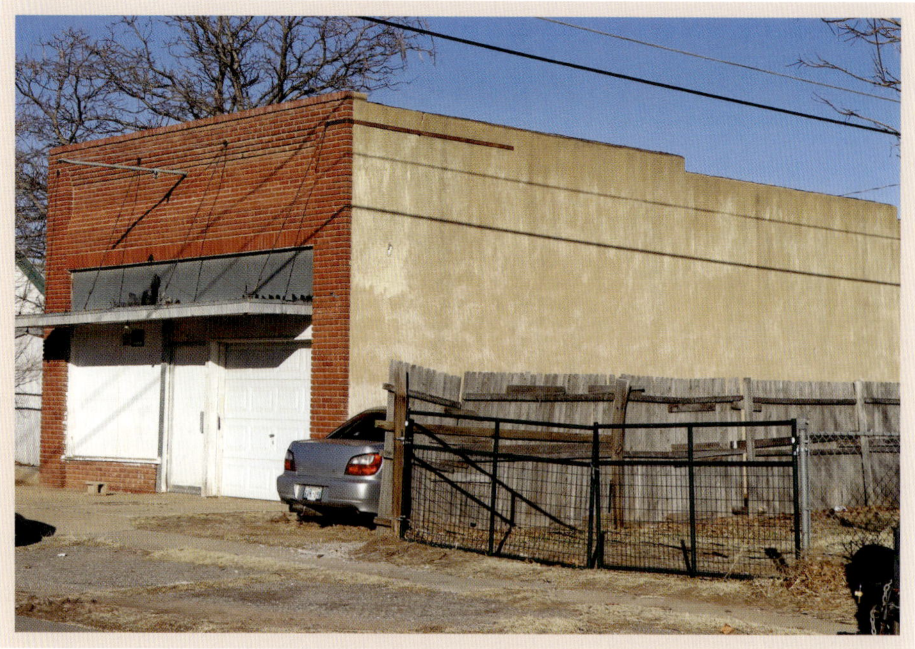

This photograph of the Bassett Grocery at 516 Oak Avenue in Woodward dates to the mid-1930s. Standing on the porch, from left to right, are Emma Bassett, Maxine (Basset) Culp, Bert Bassett, and Cordy Rose. By the late 1940s, the store was owned by Orrie and Ruth Booze and called Orrie's. Regardless of ownership, the store was always known for its lunch counter and was a popular hangout for school kids in the afternoon. The building is privately owned today.

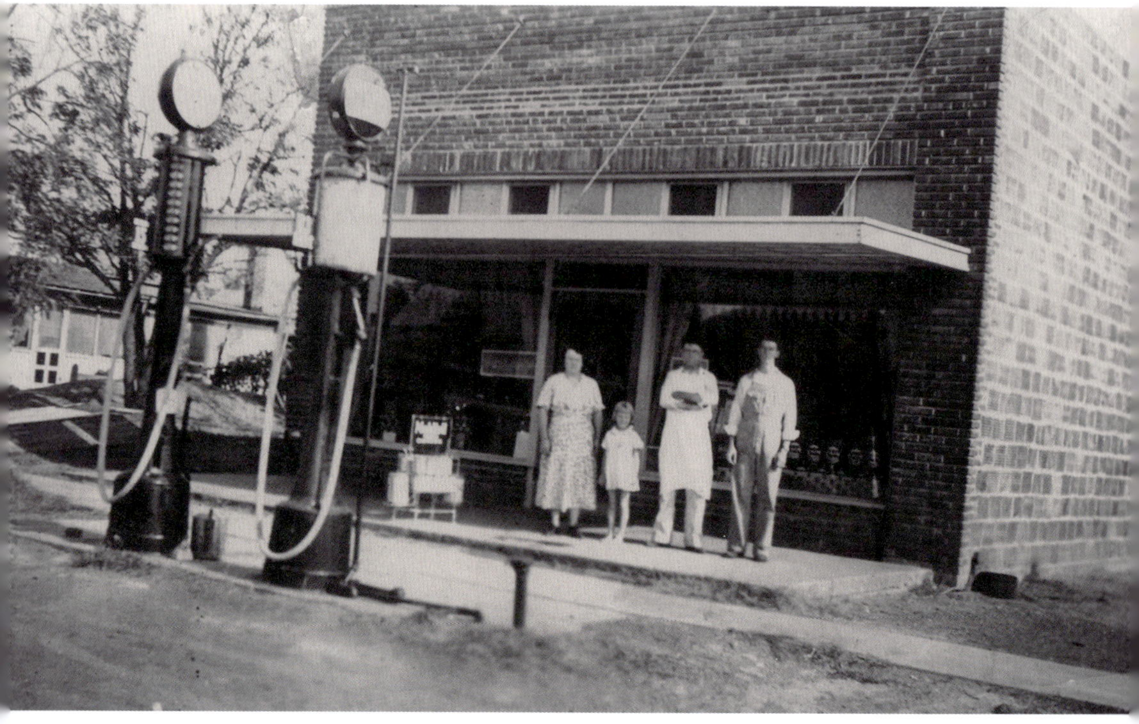

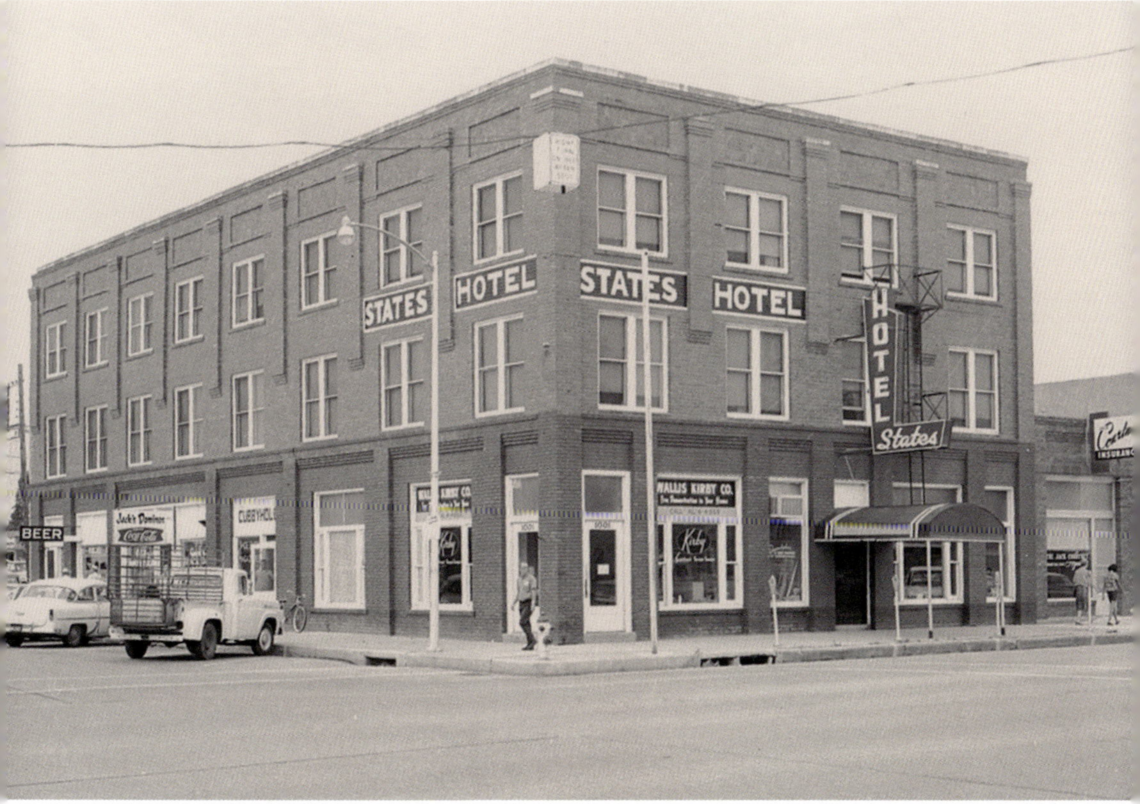

The original two-story structure on the southwest corner of Tenth and Main Streets was built in 1904 by William Ezra "Billy" Bolton, editor/publisher of the *Woodward News*. By 1925, as the Ideal Hotel, the exterior block walls were torn down, and new brick walls went up while adding a third floor. It later became the States Hotel, named for having 48 rooms, and became infamous as a brothel. The hotel closed in 1983 and then served as a chiropractic practice.

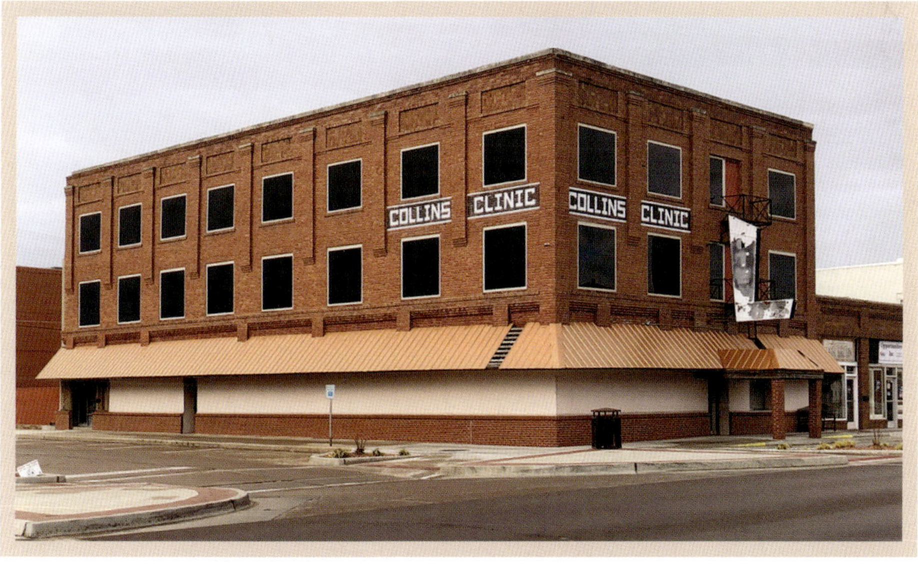

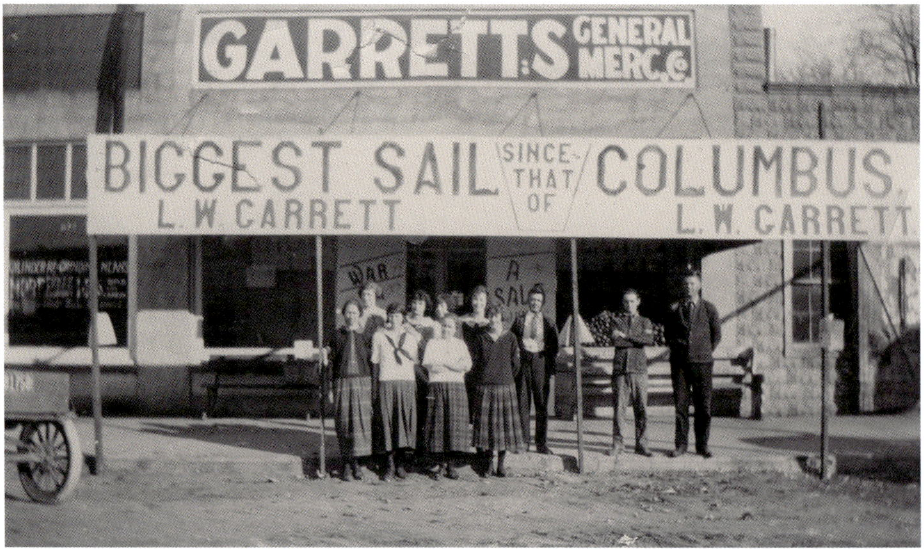

Garrett's General Mercantile Co. was at 520 Main Street and owned by L.W. Garrett (at far right). At the time the photograph was taken in 1920, the store was running its Columbus Day "Sail." Garrett had a sense of humor. The photograph below shows the approximate site of the original store, currently housing an auto accessory shop.

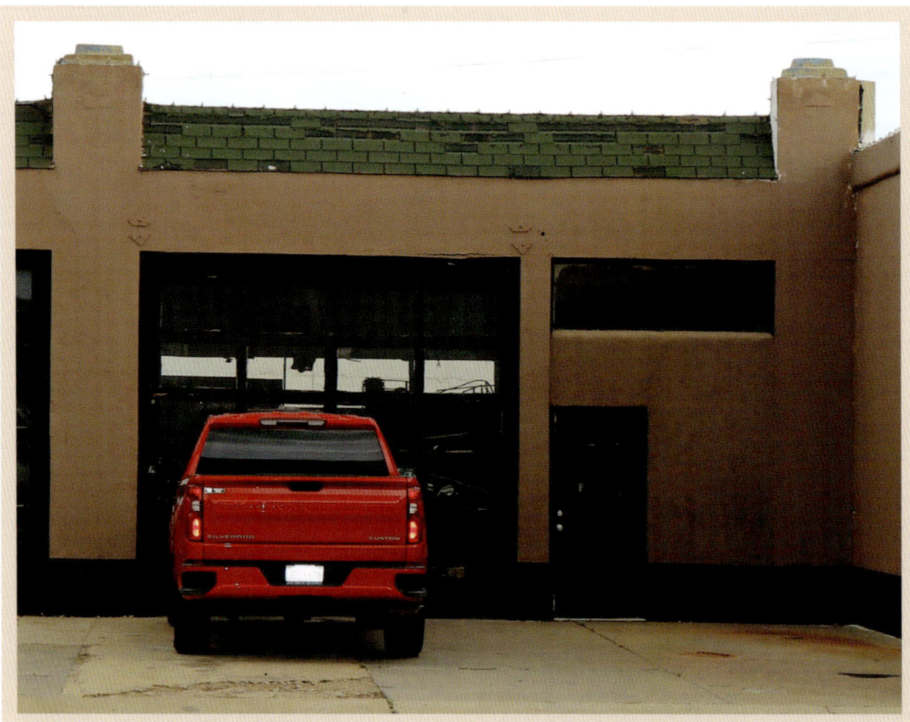

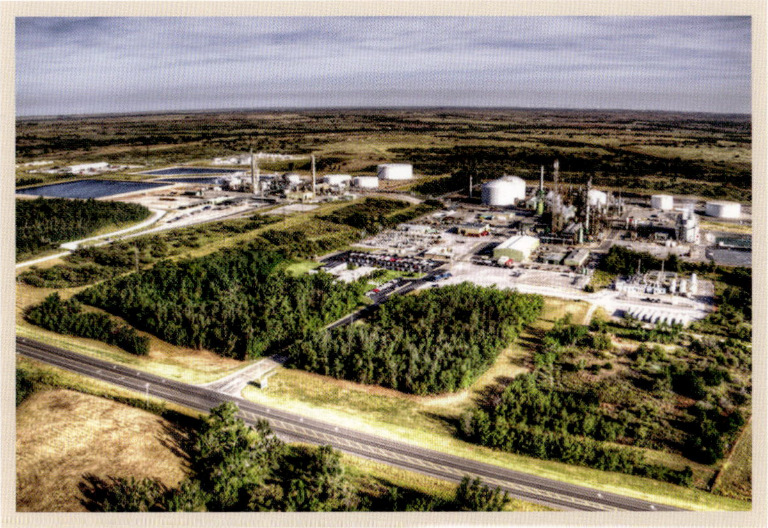

Begun with the excavation of a site west of Woodward, the Oklahoma Nitrogen Company was a joint venture of W.R. Grace, Gulf Oil Chemicals, and Terra Chemicals. By August 1978, the business was producing urea ammonium nitrate. In 1988, Terra Nitrogen became the sole owner until 2010, when CF Industries purchased Terra. The CF Industries' Woodward Nitrogen Complex has the capacity to produce one million tons of nitrogen fertilizer annually. (Above, courtesy of CF Industries.)

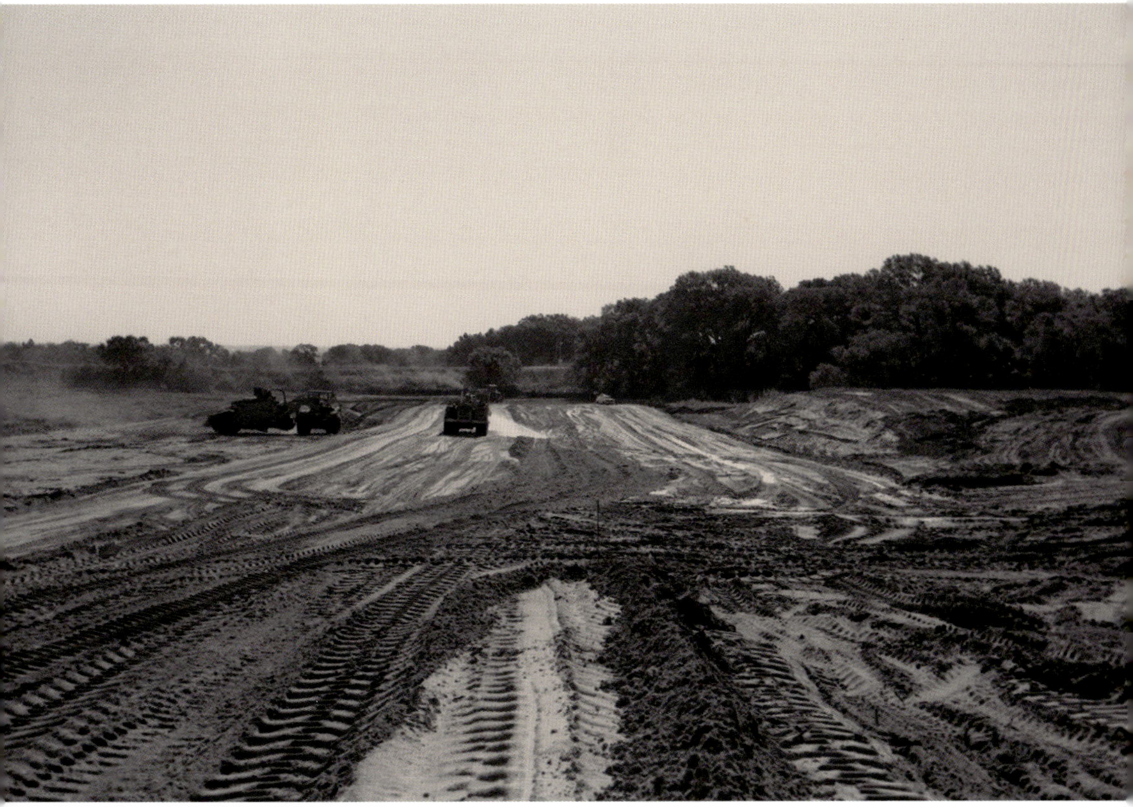

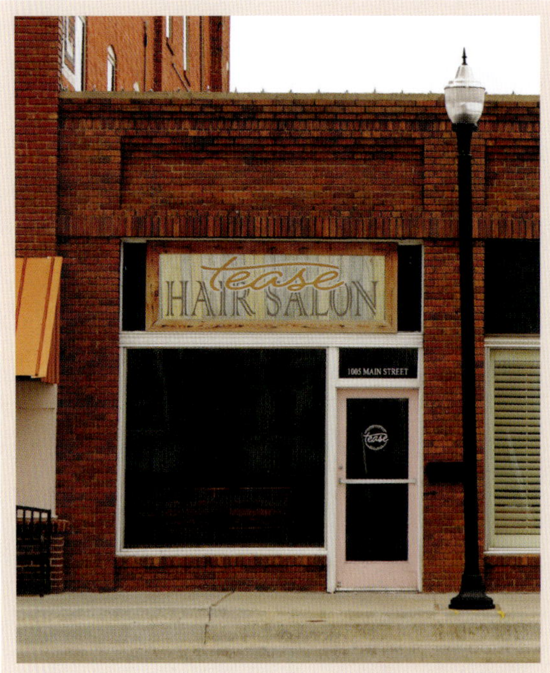

The image below shows the Guy O. Duggin Grocery Co. in the early 1900s when it was on the south side of Main Street at 1005. Duggin's store remained here until the 1920s, when his son F.L. Duggin opened a grocery on Texas Avenue and Guy Duggin went to work as a clerk for his son. The original structure is gone, but the modern photograph is in close proximity to the original site.

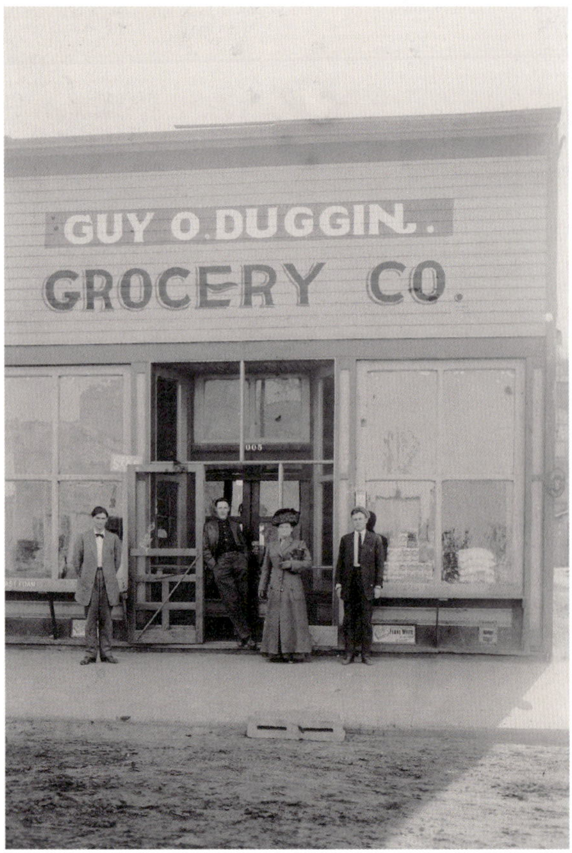

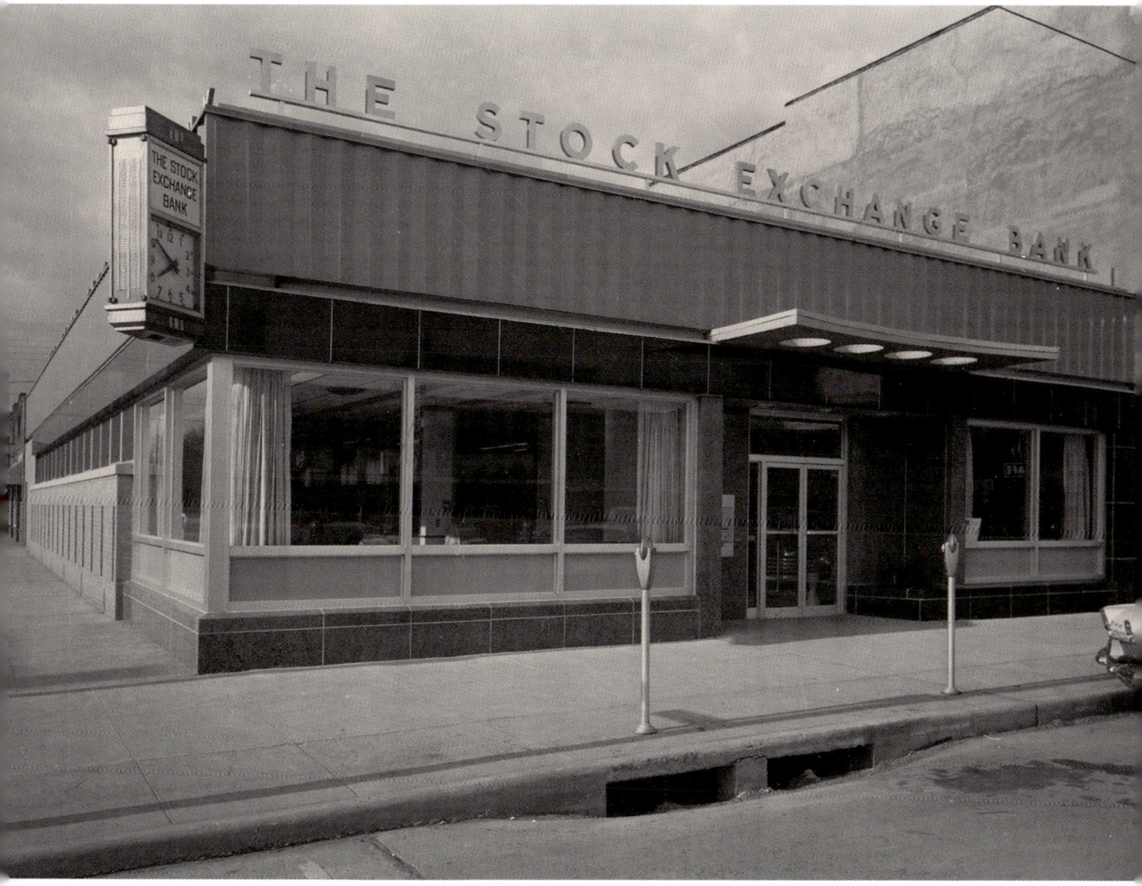

Originally founded in January 1903 in Oleta, Oklahoma Territory (present-day Fargo), the Stock Exchange Bank moved to Woodward in June 1939. The first location of the bank was at 907 Main Street, but it moved next door when a new building was constructed (shown here) in October 1959. Although the main bank branch is no longer on Main Street, the building remains in the Benbrook family as the Benbrook Insurance Agency.

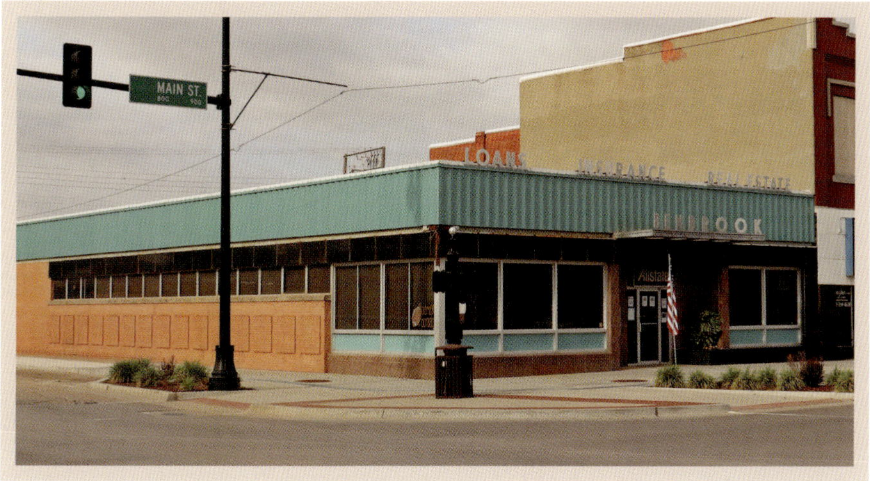

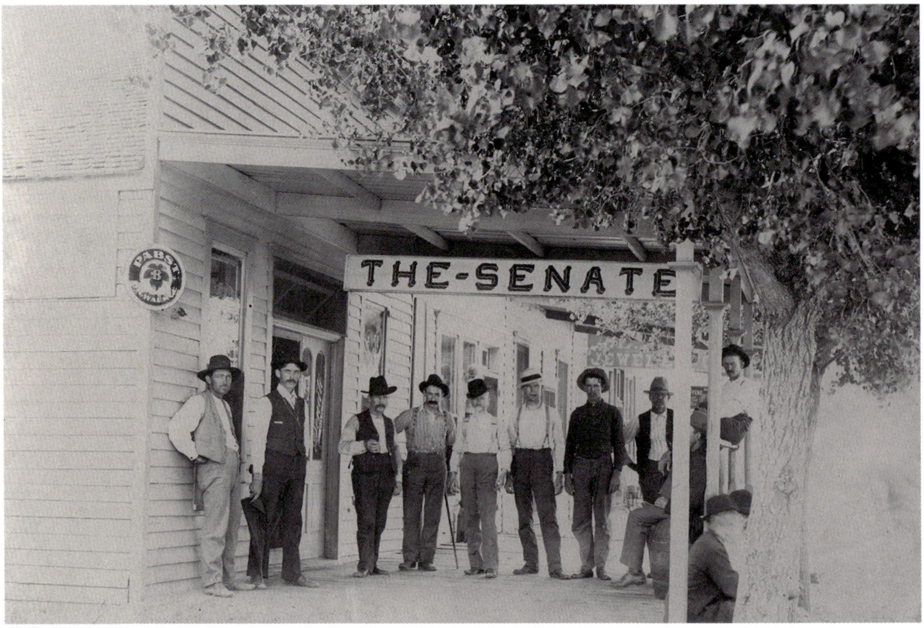

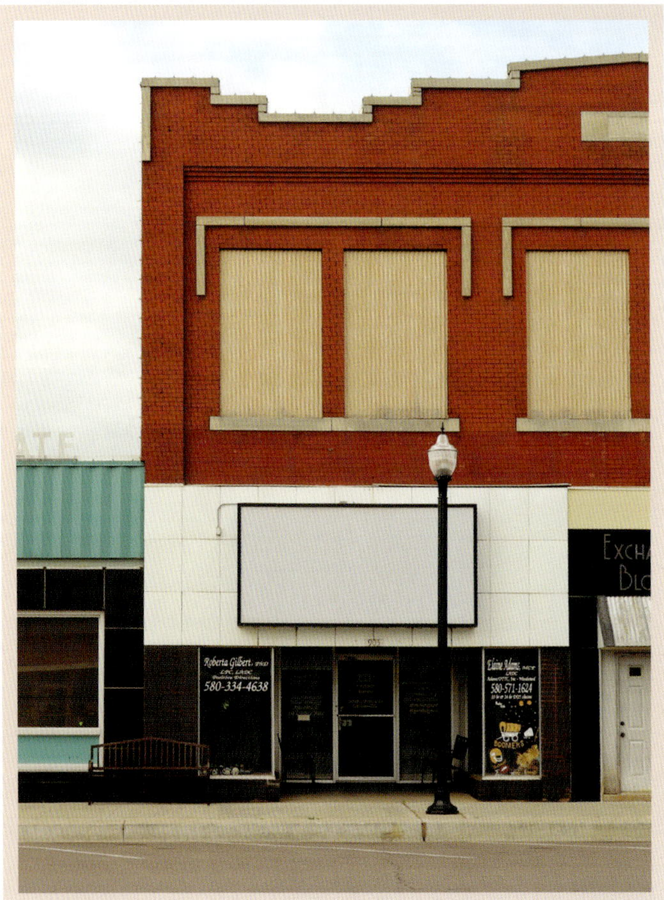

It is said that there were more saloons, brothels, and dance halls than any other "legitimate" business in territorial Woodward. This photograph of the Senate Saloon at 905 Main Street shows some of that establishment's customers posing outside. Although the photograph is undated, the fact that none of the men are wearing a sidearm would indicate it is likely the late 1890s or early 1900s. The location is now a counseling services practice.

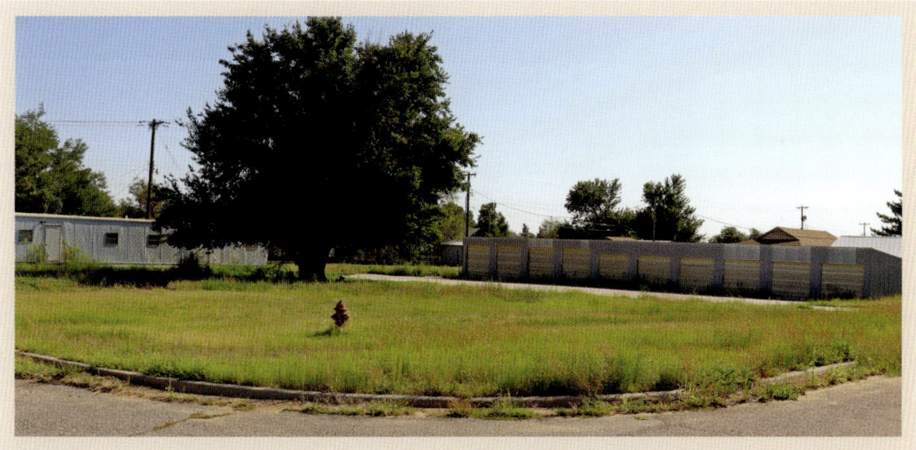

This photograph of the Bowlin Broom Company probably dates to around 1920. C.E. Bowlin bought out his partner W.C. Walker in 1916 and made it his own. At the time of the dissolution, Walker indicated he was retiring. By at least 1925, Walker was in direct competition with his former partner doing business as Walker Broom Factory. In 1925, the chamber of commerce reported that the two factories were producing 154,080 brooms a year.

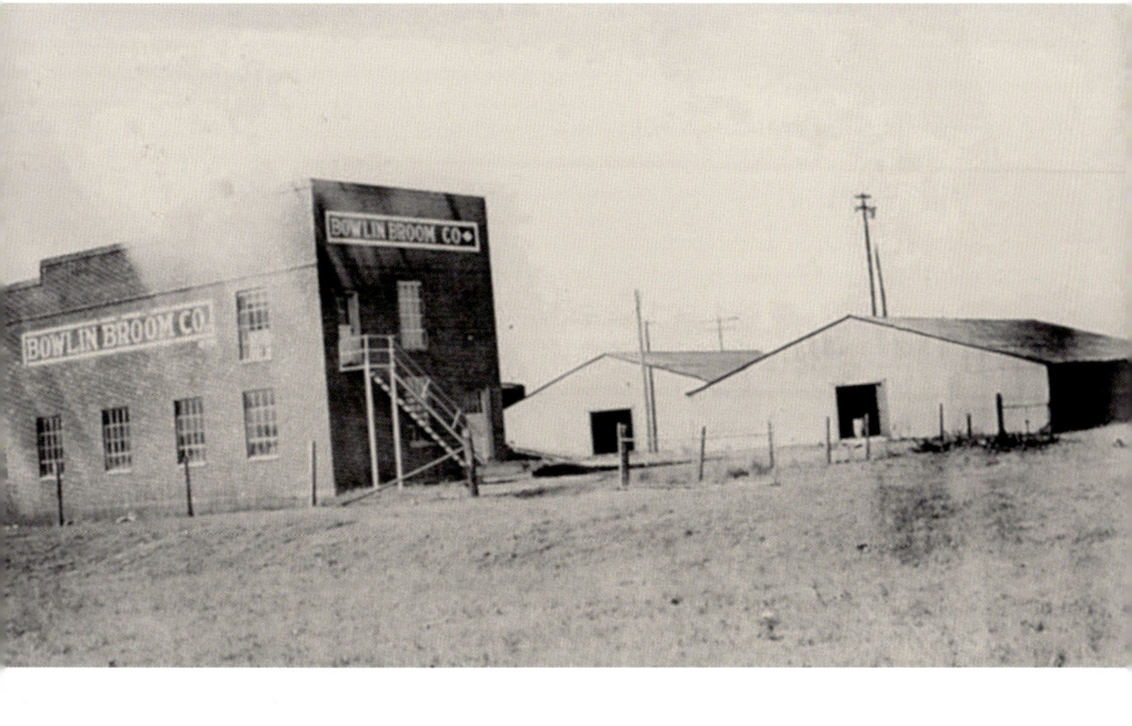

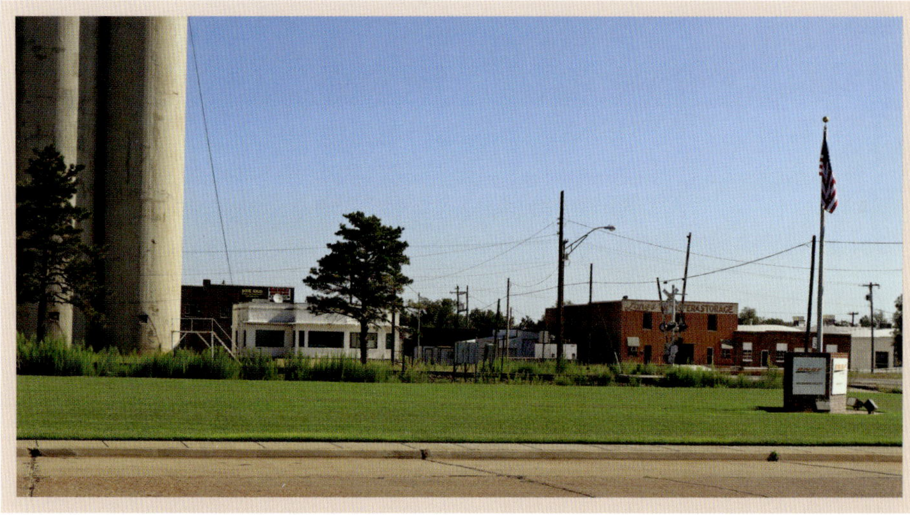

C.A. Hoops Grain and Coal Co. was owned and operated by C.A. Hoops, who came to Woodward with the opening of the Cherokee Outlet in 1893. Hoops apparently had a sense of humor—note the elk to his right, which was likely placed there for the photograph as it does not appear in any other photographs of the business. His advertising always featured a "devil-ish" figure as a testament to how hot his coal lumps were.

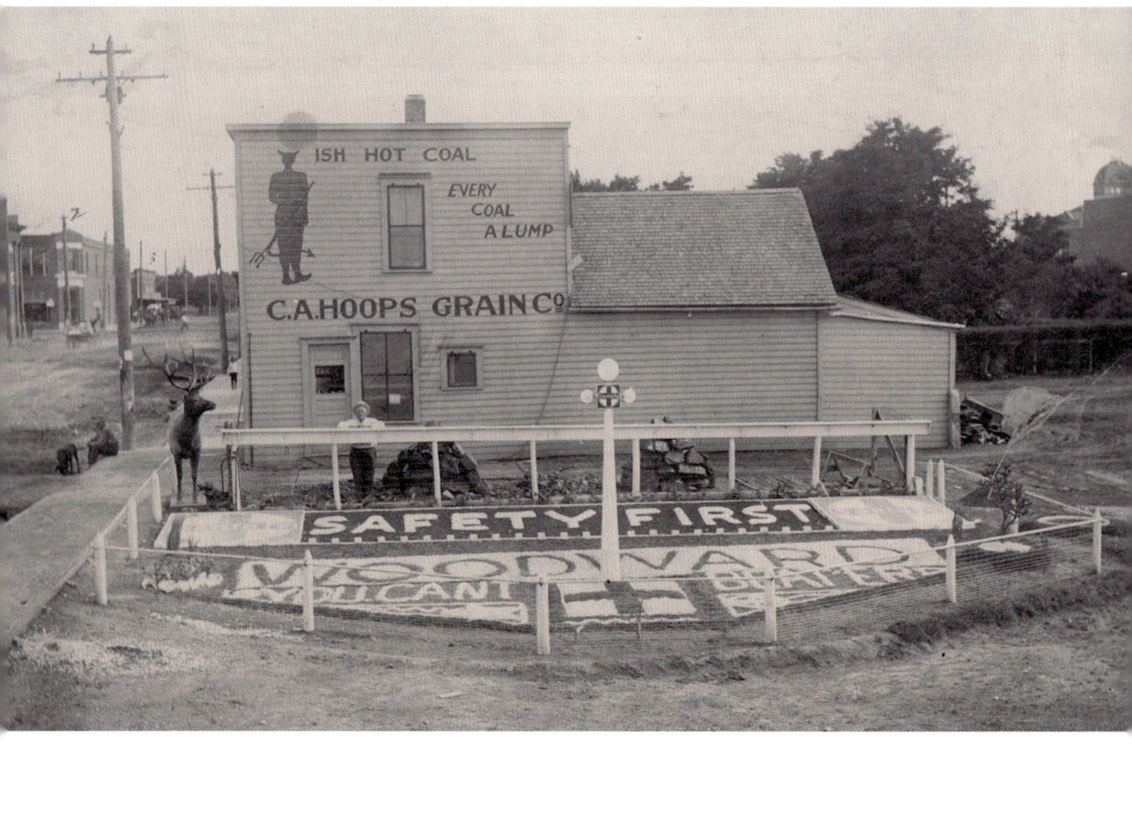

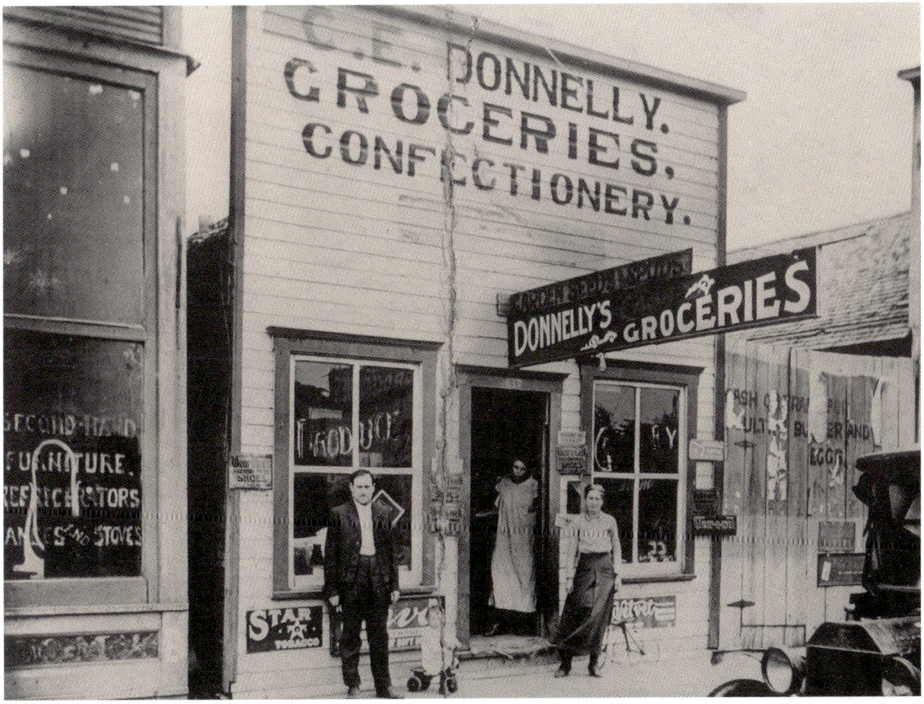

The photograph from 1915 shows Donnelly's groceries and confectionery at 617 Main Street, the present-day location of KenKool Heat and Air. The owner, Curtis Donnelly, is at far left. The child is Gerald Avery Donnelly. The woman on the sidewalk is Quintilla Parks Donnelly. Bertha Smith Donnelly, Curtis's mother, is standing in the doorway. The store operated in this location from 1910 to 1920.

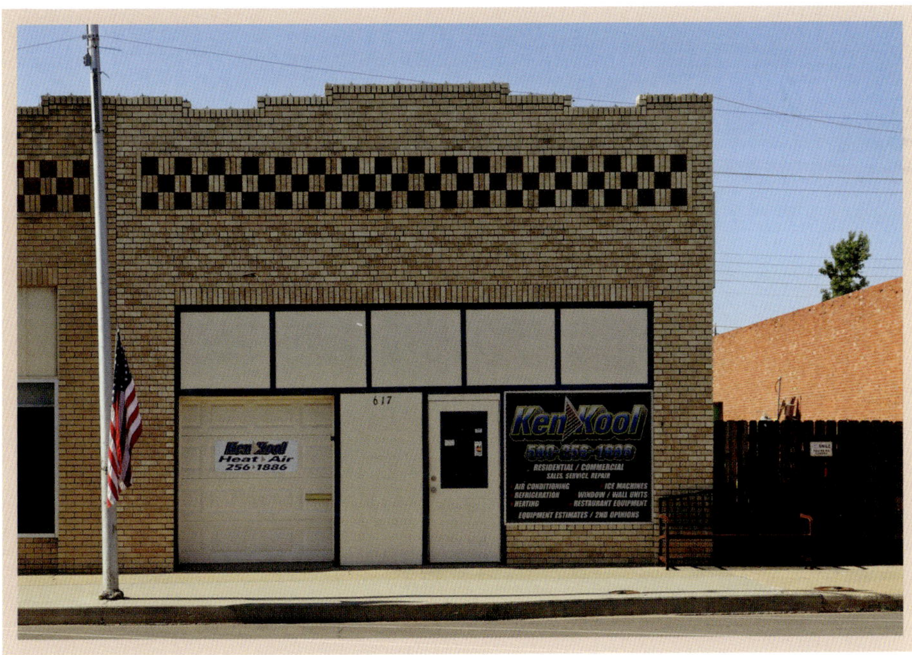

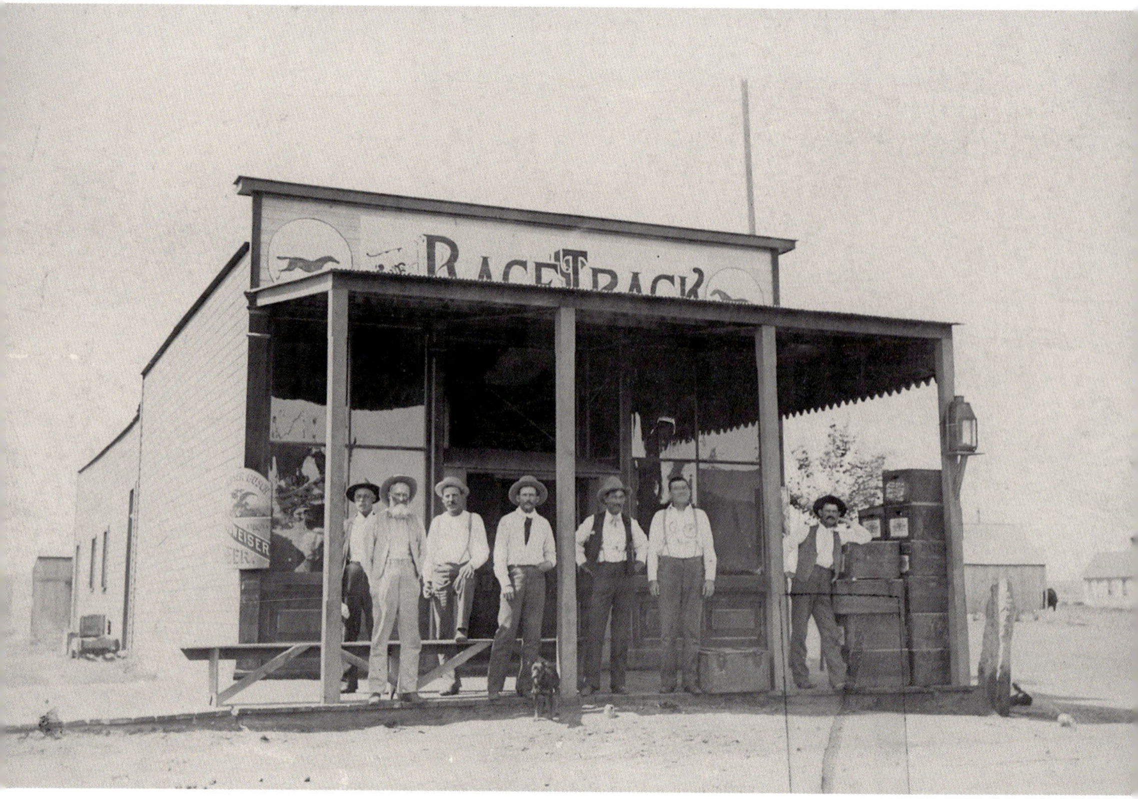

Located on the southeast corner of Tenth and Main Streets, the RaceTrack Saloon provided the first opportunity for a refreshing beverage for anyone coming into town from the west. The photograph dates to around 1900. The RaceTrack advertised "ice cold lemonade, beer and fancy drinks of every description, from amontillado wine down to fighting whiskey." Over the years, the location was used for a variety of automobile services, and today is home to Five-Star Biz.

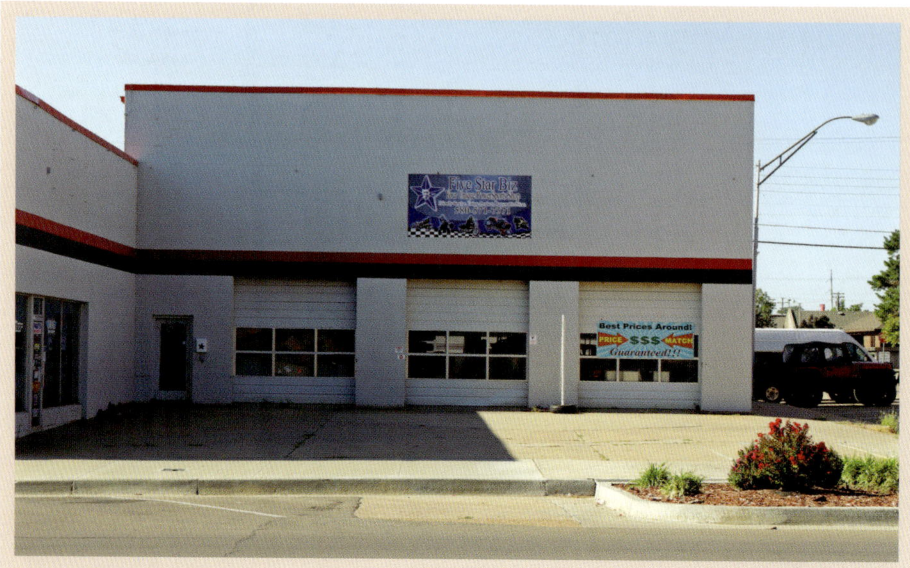

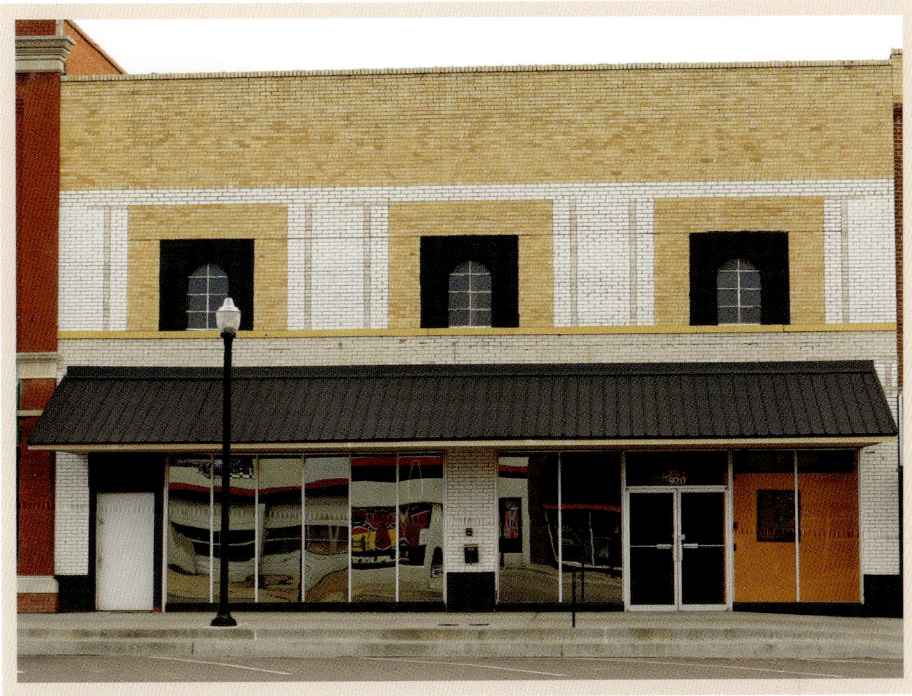

The Orpheum Theatre at 920 Main Street was owned and operated by Harry Johnson. The Gaskins Family Band became the house band for the theater. The unusual shell-shaped entrance to the theater is shown below. The Woodward County attorney once publicly remarked that only people of bad character attended performances at the Orpheum, which undoubtedly drove up ticket sales. The original theater building burned to the ground at some point.

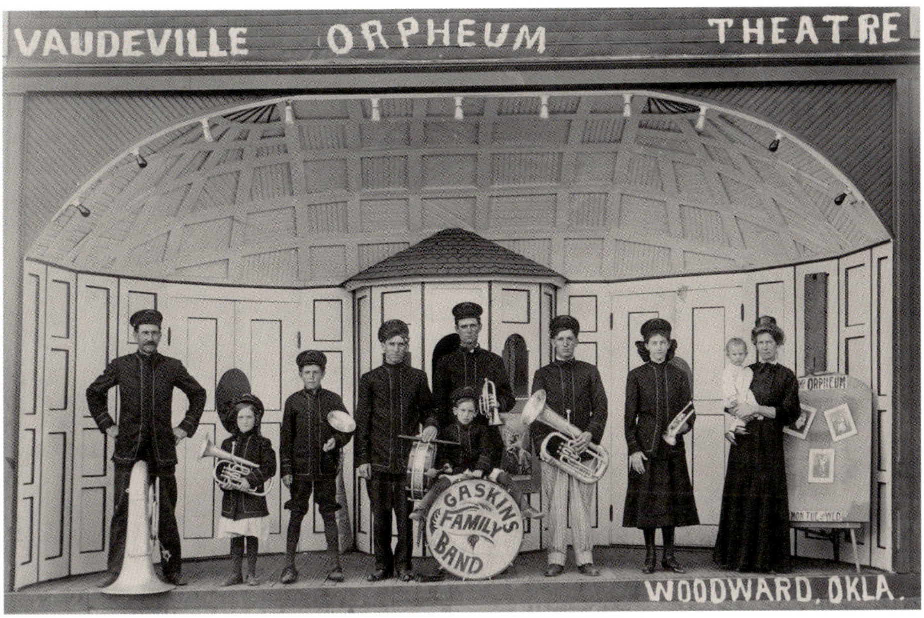

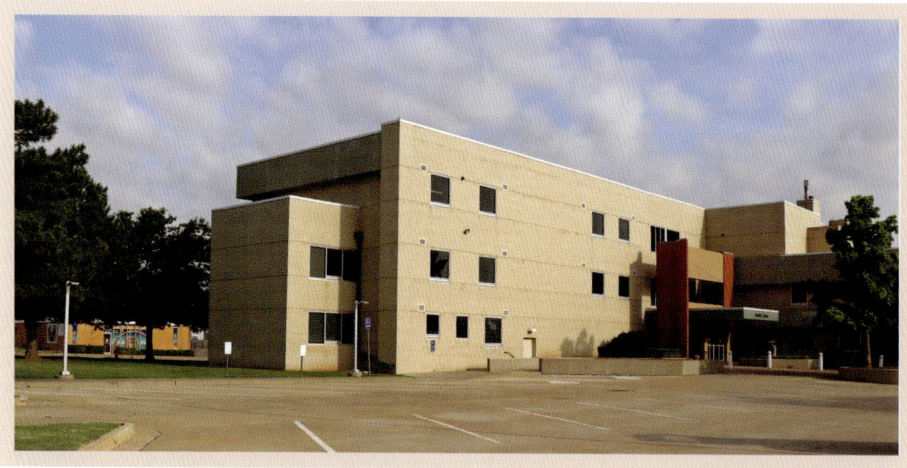

Woodward Memorial Hospital was built in 1952 in an effort to modernize healthcare services in Woodward and surrounding communities. A third floor was added in the early 1960s to increase bed and surgical capacity. A major refurbishment was undertaken in 1984 to renovate the exterior of the old building and included a major addition to the north end of the building as well as a heliport. The hospital is now operated as Alliance Health Woodward.

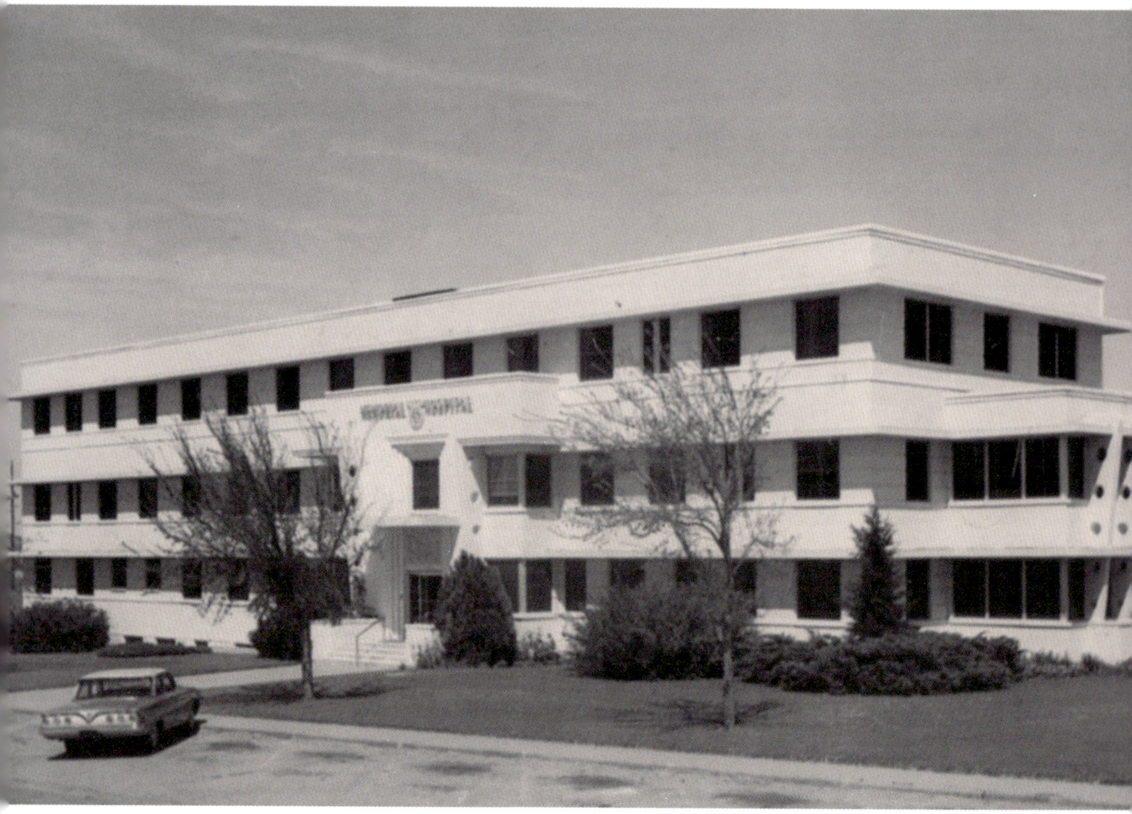

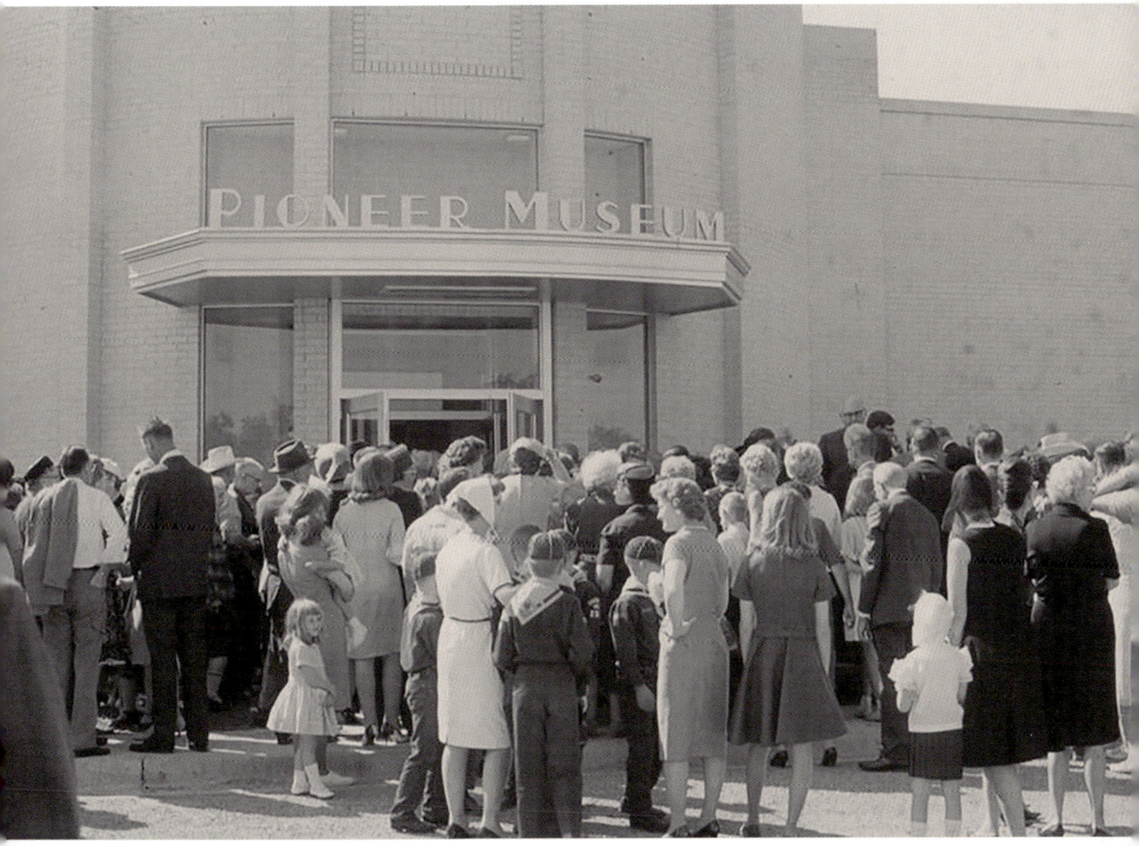

Begun as a concept by a group of dedicated volunteers, the Plains Indians & Pioneers Museum opened in September 1966 as a repository for the history and artifacts of northwest Oklahoma. The organization has served the region for more than a half century, with thousands of visitors every year. There is an art gallery featuring a constantly rotating display of works by Oklahoma artists. Programming provides an educational resource for Woodward and surrounding counties.

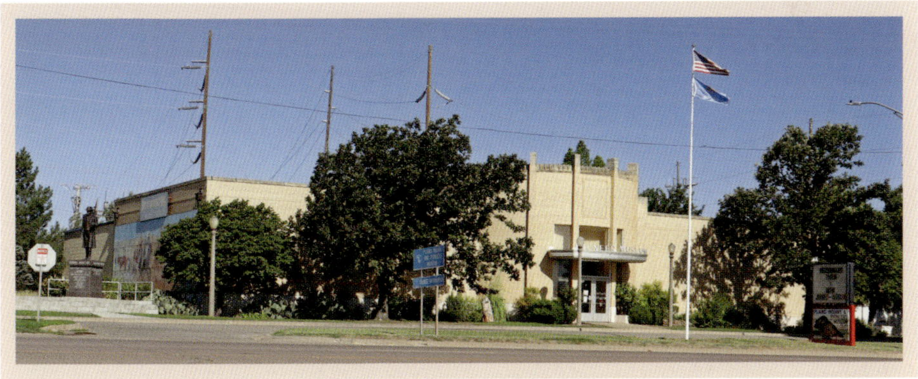

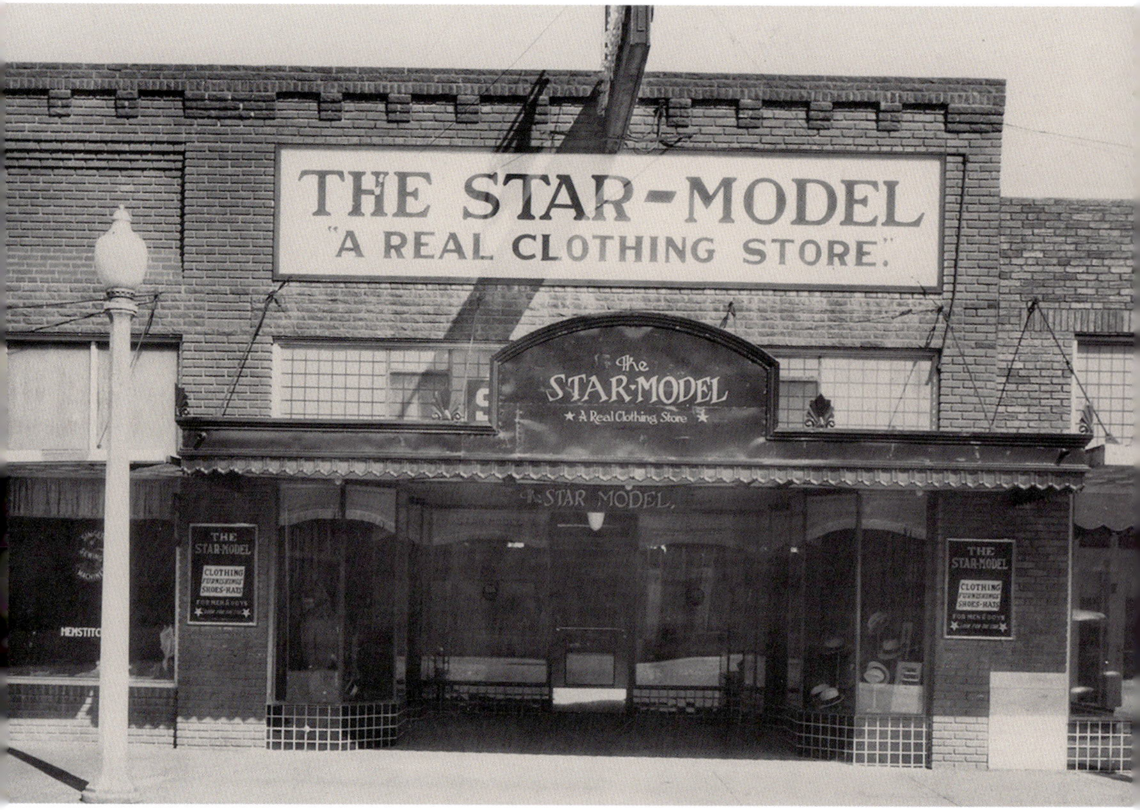

The Star Model store (originally the Star Clothing Store) was a major retail anchor for the north side of the 900 block of Main Street from the early 1900s, giving it near landmark status. Despite changes in ownership over the decades, the store remained a steady source of quality men's clothing and provided many high school kids with part-time jobs. The Persimmon Creek store now occupies the same building.

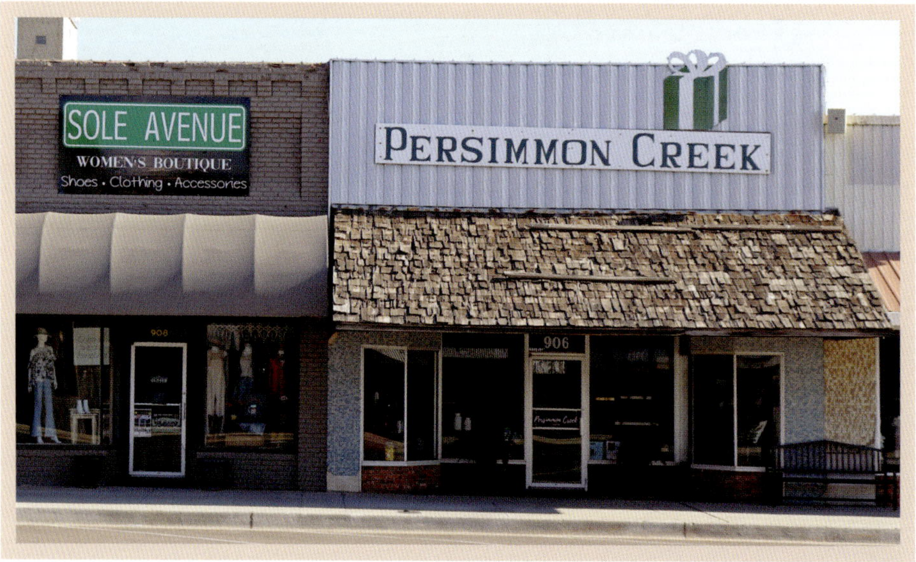

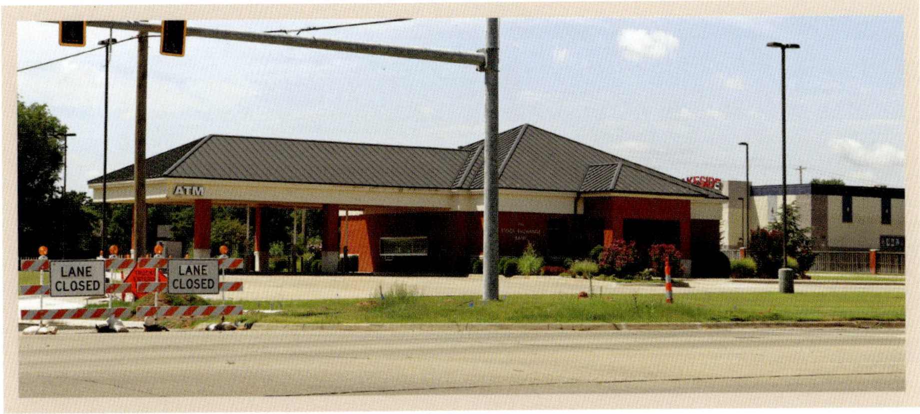

The vintage photograph of the Terrytime drive-in theater was taken soon after an incredible snowstorm in March 1971. The Terrytime was another jewel in the crown of movie theaters owned and operated by the Terry family of Woodward. It opened on April 25, 1950, with a capacity of 416 cars. The long-closed site was demolished in the mid-2000s to make way for another branch of the Stock Exchange Bank.

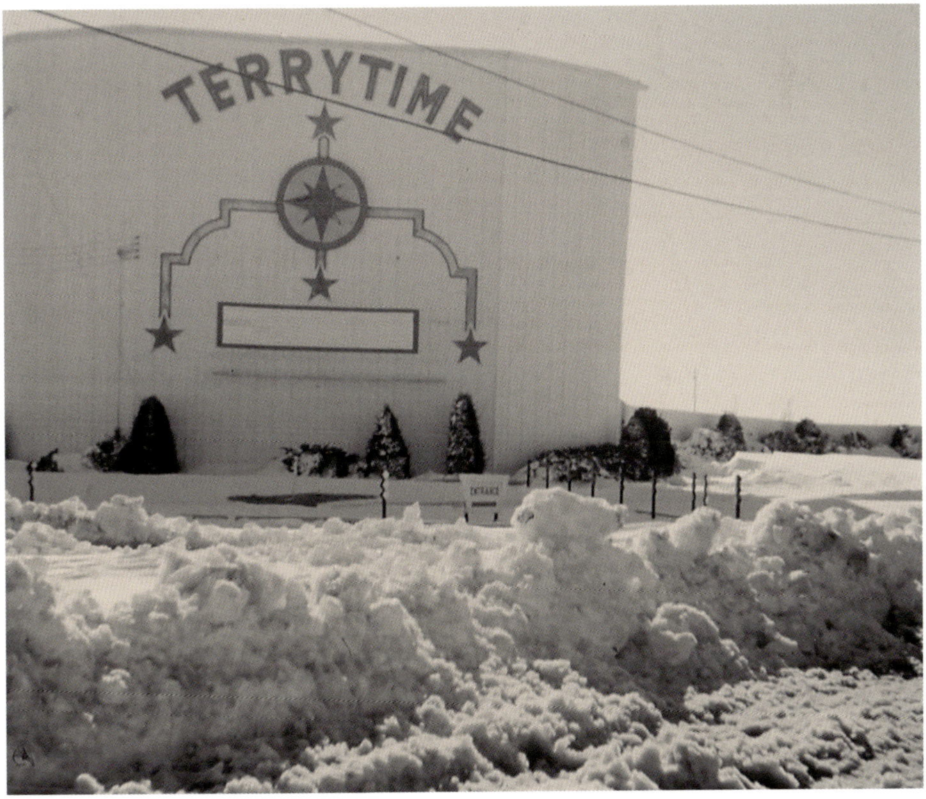

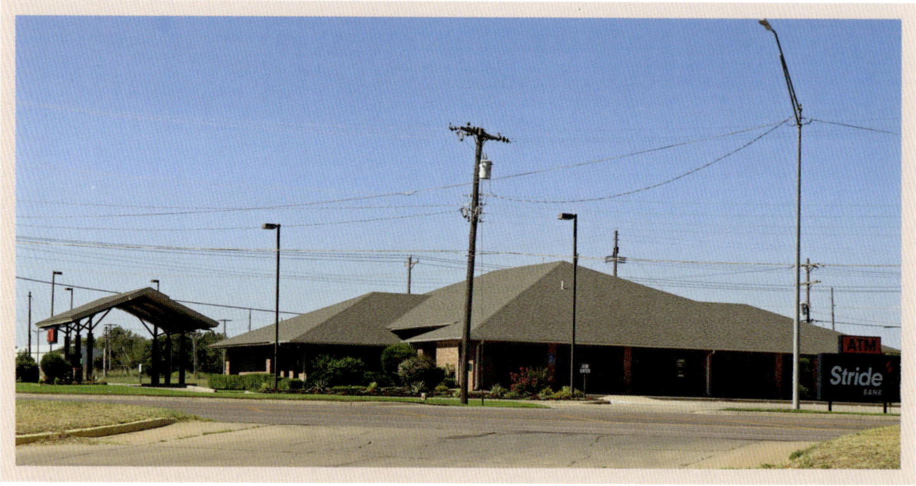

The undated photograph of the former location of VFW Post 1335 at Ninth Street and Downs Avenue shows a rather empty area south of town. The building was known for being a dance hall, with dances at least once a week for as long as the place was open. It is reported there were a few slot machines in the back, strictly for entertainment purposes of its veteran members, of course. The site is now the location of Stride Bank.

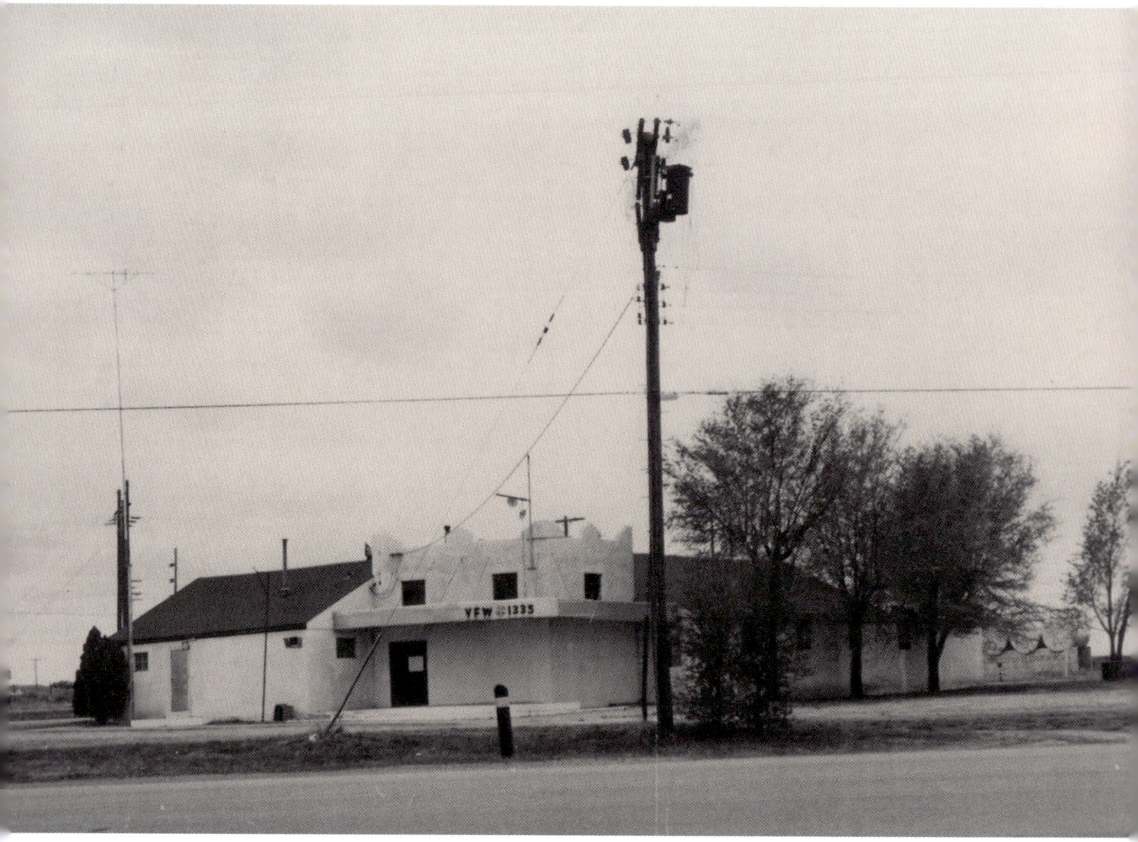

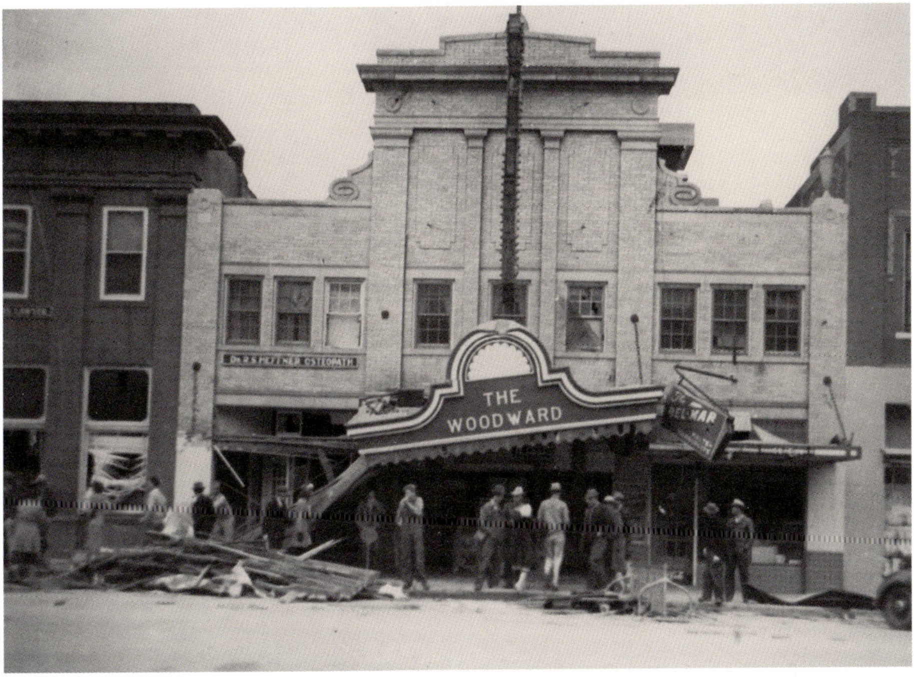

Built in 1929, the Woodward Theatre was owned by the Terry family. The financial backer for the movie house insisted that a full stage and orchestra pit be included in the build. He believed that moving pictures were a passing fad. The vintage photograph shows the aftermath of the 1947 tornado. The building underwent a major restoration in 1981, reopening as the Woodward Arts Theatre. It remains in use today as a lively arts venue.

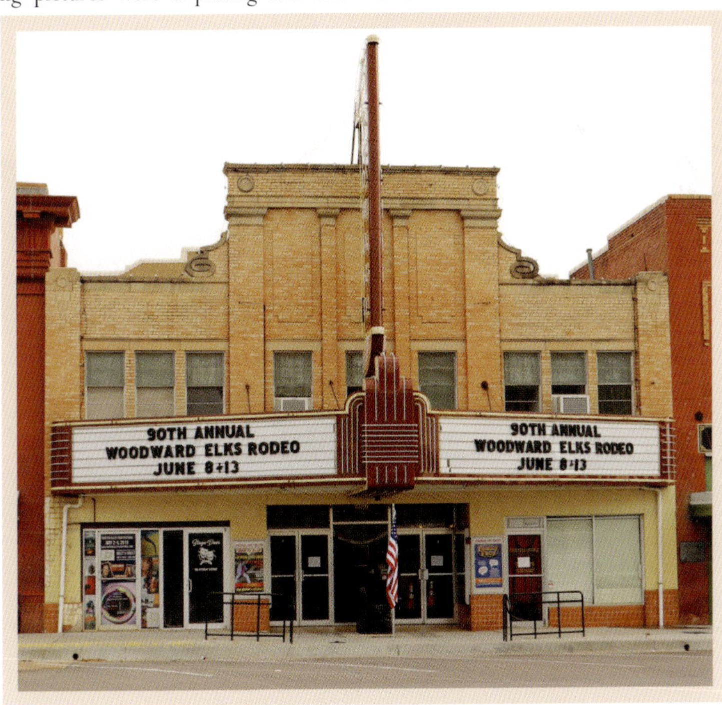

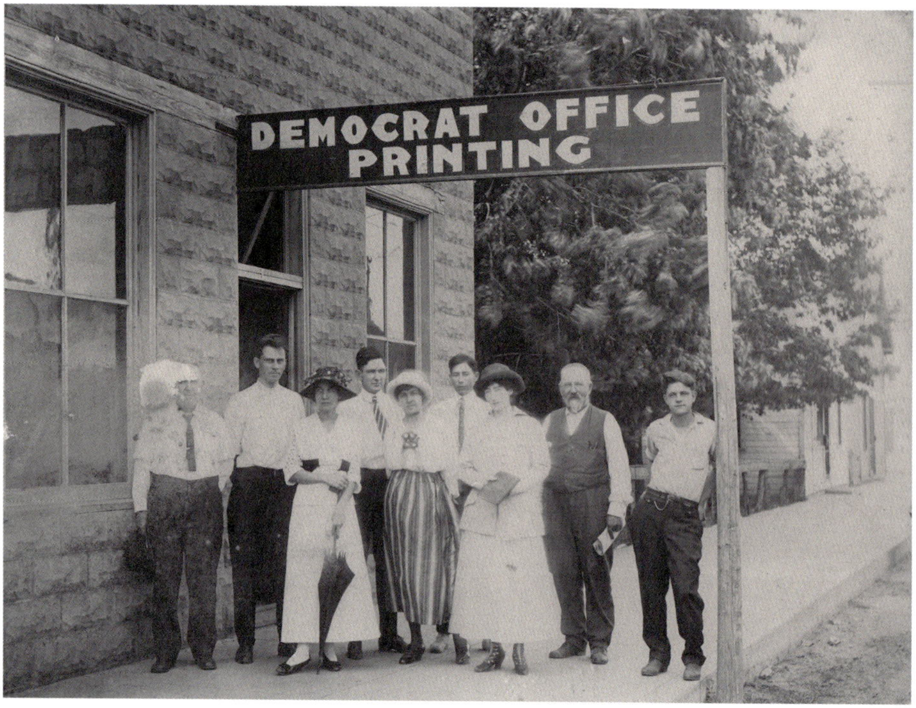

This photograph of the home of the *Woodward Daily Democrat* dates to 1917. From left to right are L.B. Collins, Harvey Bull, unidentified, Clark Lawrence (later publisher of the *Woodward Daily Press*), Lela Bell Young, Judge David Marum (editor/publisher of the *Democrat*), and Ted Taylor. Marum loomed large as a pioneer lawyer (law partner with Temple Houston) and judge. He was instrumental in the establishment of the USDA field station and the federal courthouse in Woodward.

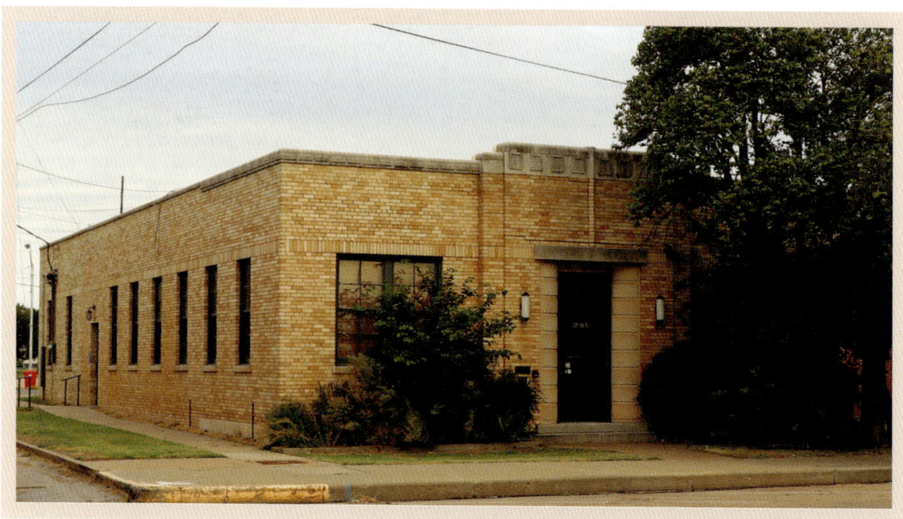

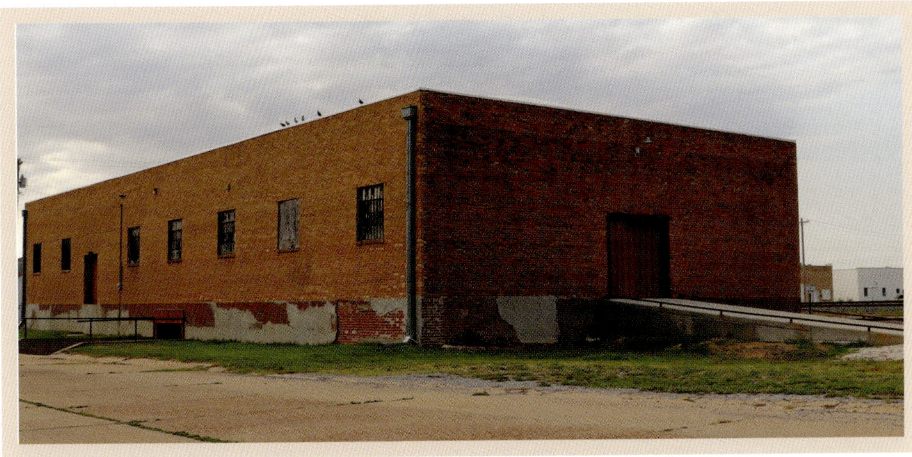

The undated photograph of Armour Creameries at 623 Santa Fe Avenue probably dates to the 1920s, based on the vehicles seen around it. The creamery was reduced to rubble in the 1947 tornado and was rebuilt on the same location.

Producing cream was big business in Woodward in the early 20th century. A 1925 report issued by the local chamber of commerce stated that 13 million pounds of cream were shipped out of Woodward the previous year.

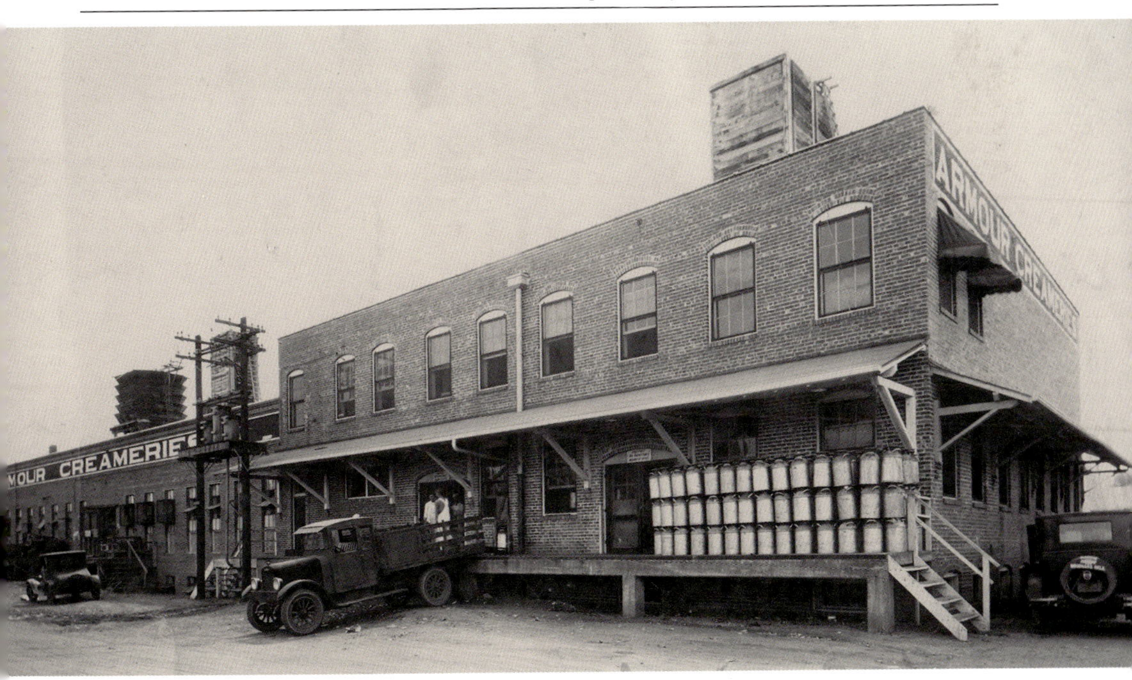

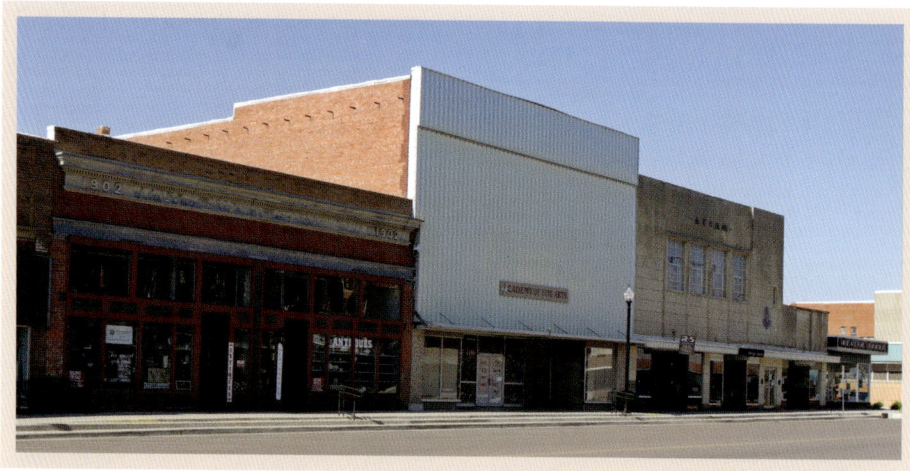

Both photographs show the south side of the 800 block of Main Street from about mid-block. The first store on the left below is Bogdahn Drug, followed by the J.C. Penney store. Next to that, in the Masonic Building, is Trego's Clothing, followed by Oliver Shoes and Frost's Store on the corner of Ninth and Main Streets. Although the names of the stores have changed, the buildings remain much as they were. Note the land yachts parked along the street below.

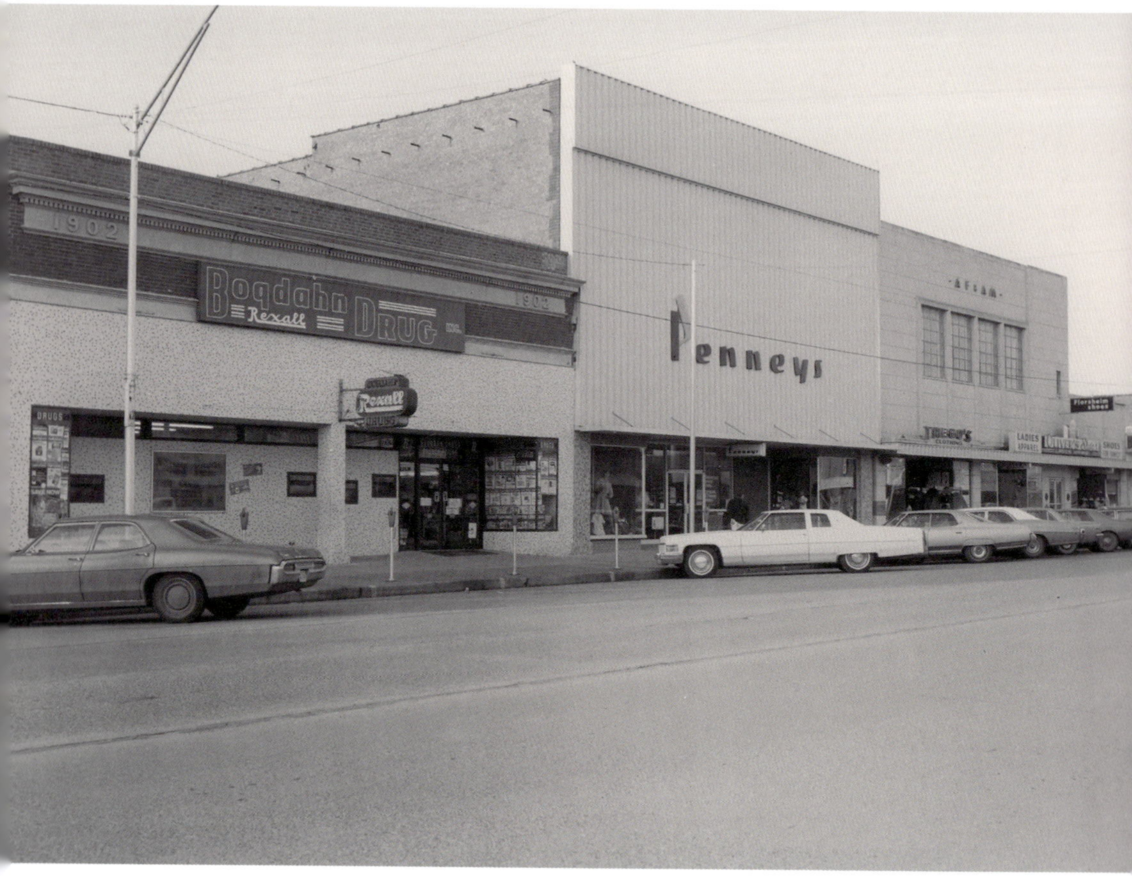

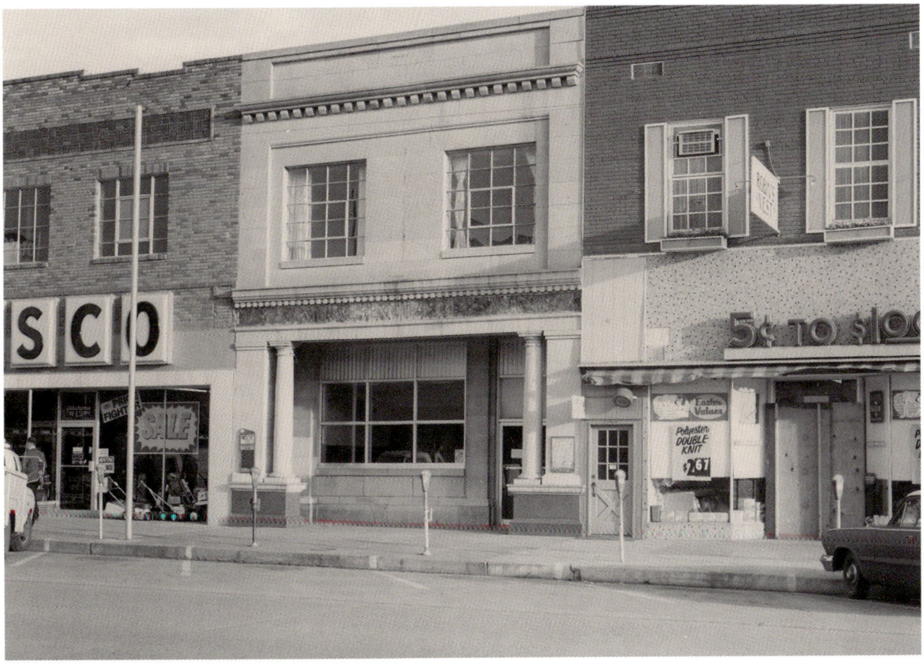

The north side of the 800 block of Main Street is shown above just after the Bank of Woodward moved down the street. The bank building (at center) was reportedly the location of the infamous Cabinet Saloon. To the left of the bank is the old OTASCO store. To the right is the entrance to the Robin's Nest, a small boutique above the old downtown location of T.G.&Y. All of these buildings are still used.

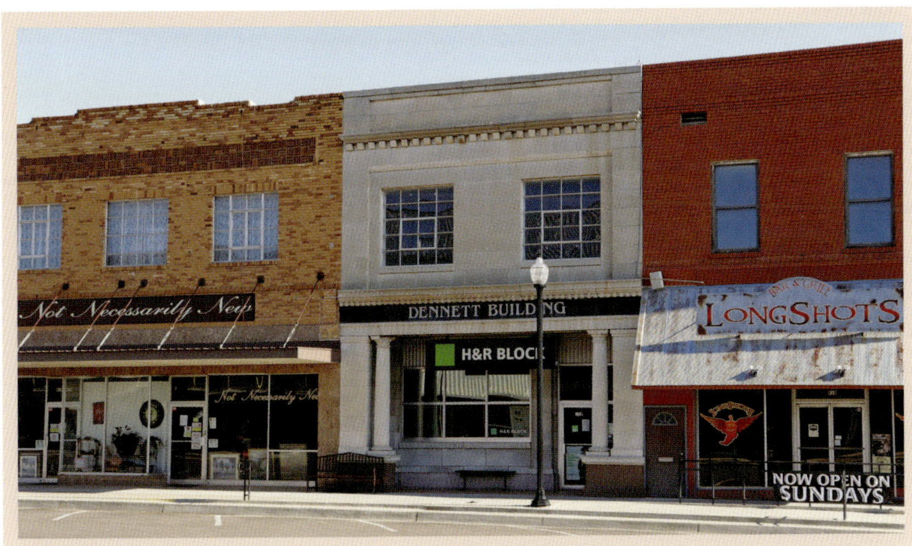

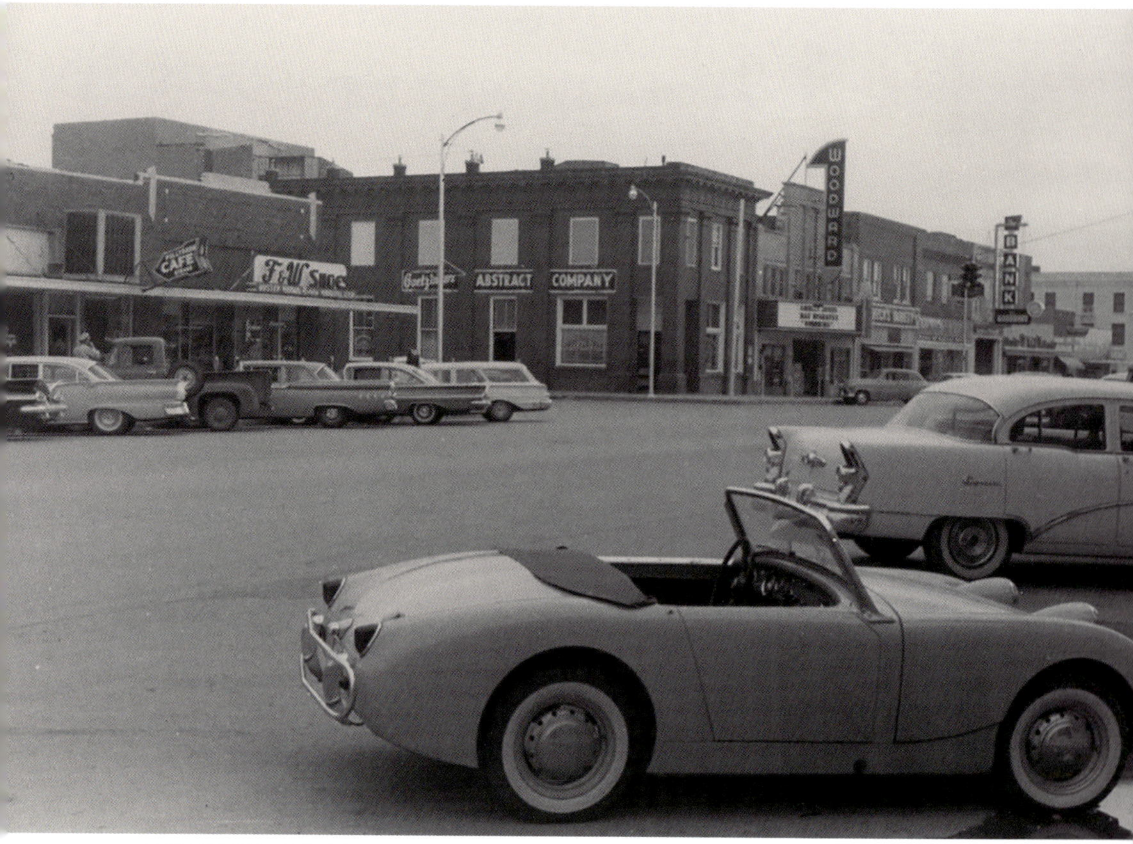

The focus of this photograph, besides the north side of Main Street, is an unusual car for Woodward in 1960, an Austin Healey Sprite. On the left is the Pollyanna Cafe, still owned by the same family. Along the 800 block is a view of the Woodward Theatre and Bank of Woodward. At far right is the Baker Hotel before it was torn down to make way for the new Bank of Woodward location.

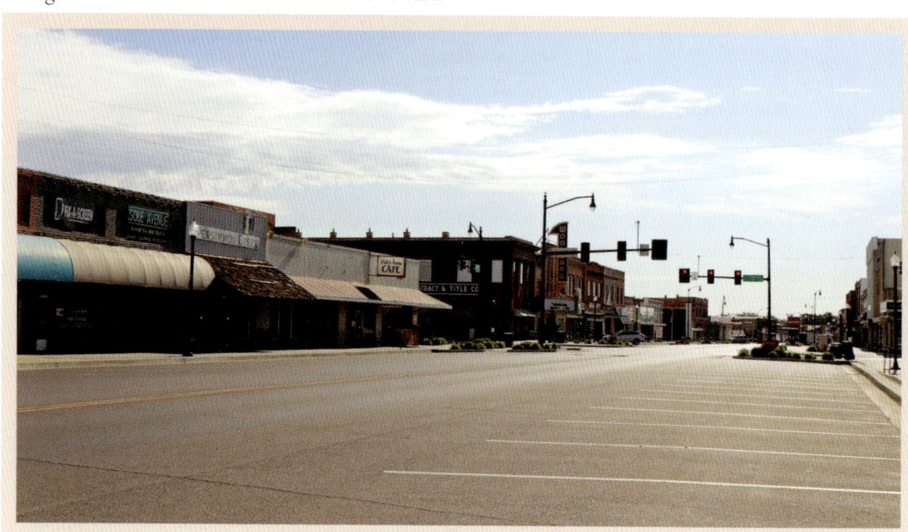

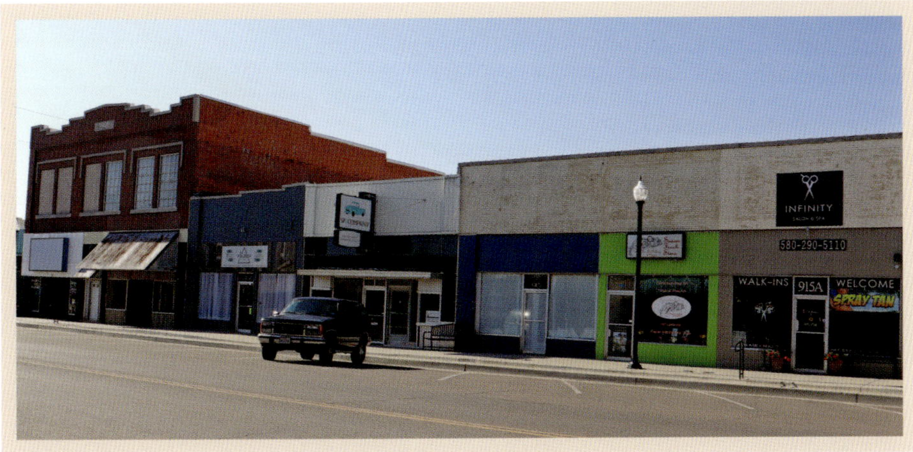

The 900 block of Main Street looking southeast is the focus of this photograph dated June 1960. The building on the left with the Stock Exchange Bank sign was the bank's first location in Woodward in 1939. By the 1960s, the 800 and 900 blocks of downtown were the center of retail in the city. Note the parking meters, a steady source of revenue for the city for many years.

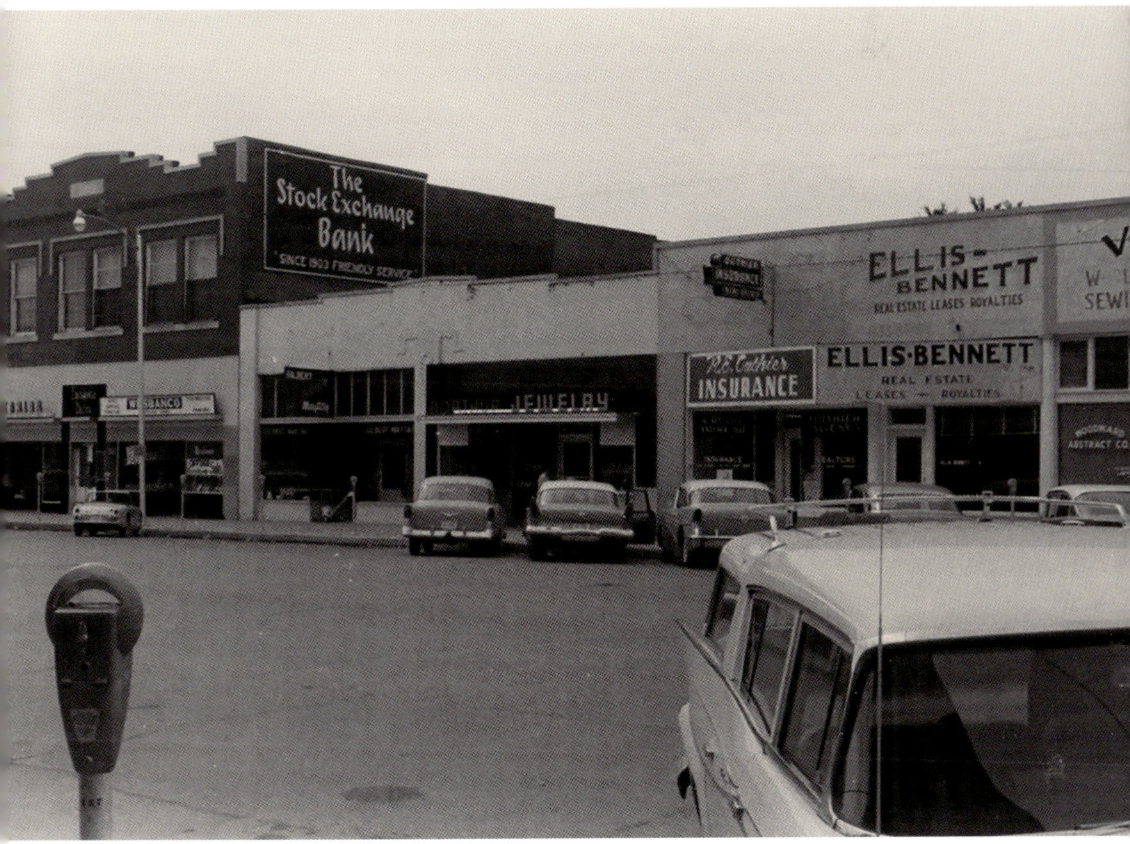

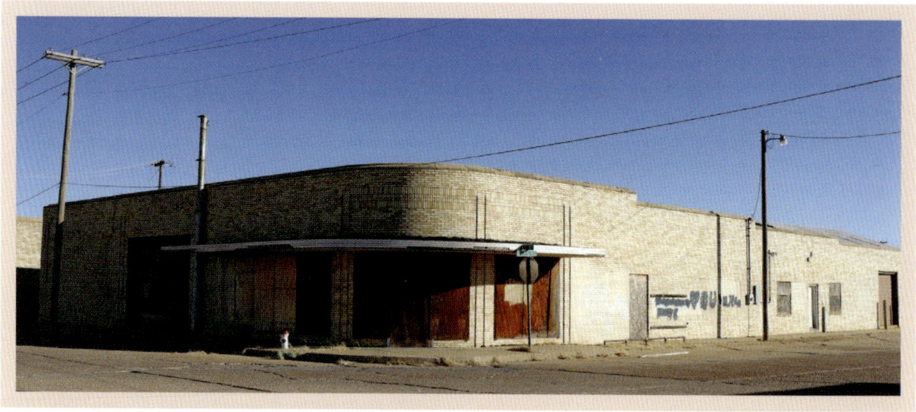

The photograph below shows the modern architecture of Osborne's Lumber (also known as Osborne-Peebles Lumber) after it was rebuilt following the 1947 tornado. The site is at the corner of Eighth Street and Santa Fe Avenue. The building was later the home of Starr Lumber, which uses the structure as a warehouse after moving its retail outlet to Main Street.

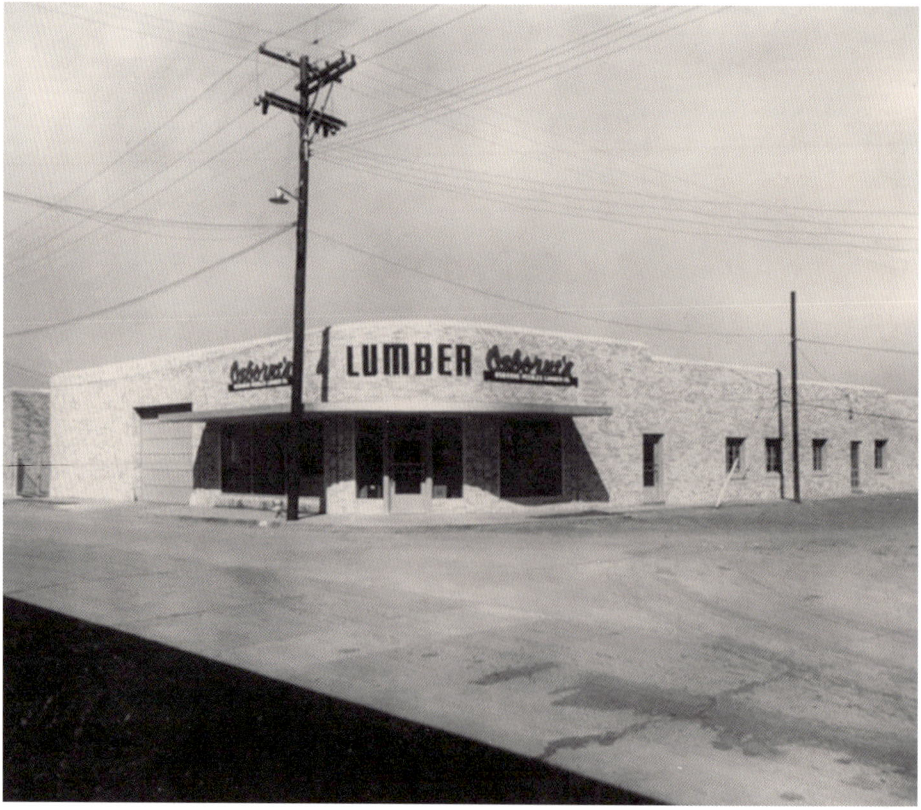

CHAPTER 2

GOVERNANCE

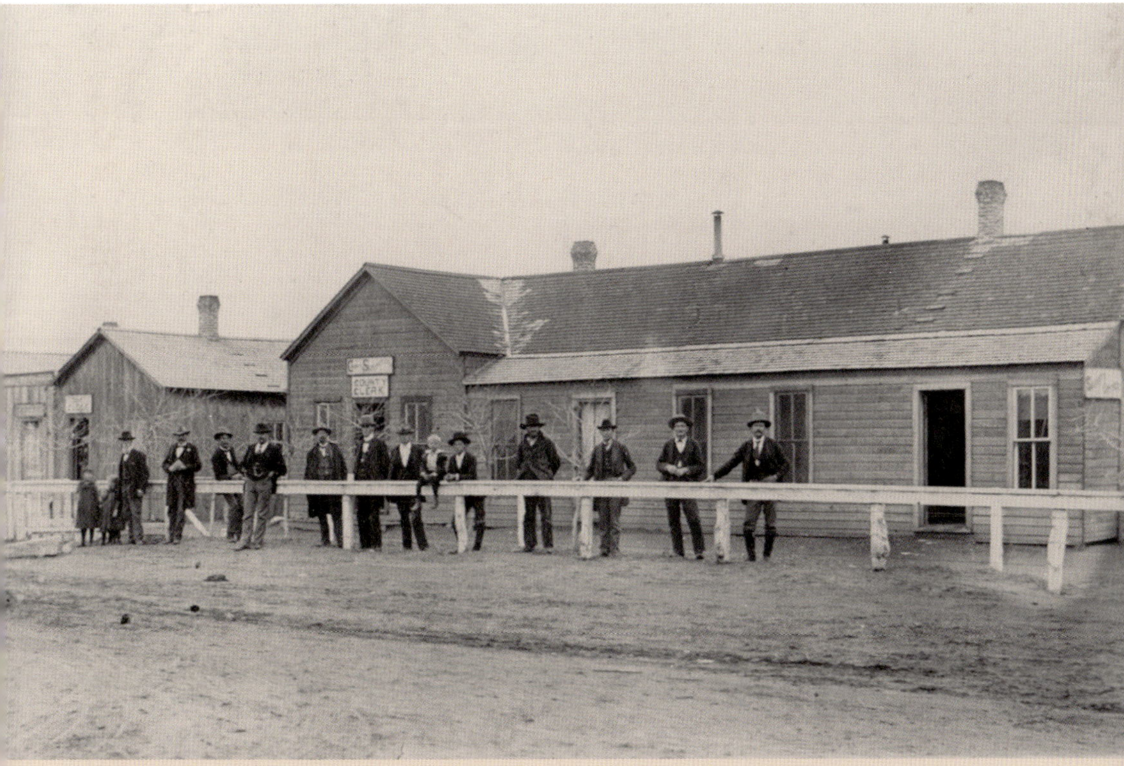

The early Woodward County complex of offices was not much more than a line of wooden buildings on the corner of Texas Avenue and Tenth Street (today the Stock Exchange Bank parking lot). The county clerk, county superintendent, and probate judge offices are all seen in this 1899 photograph.

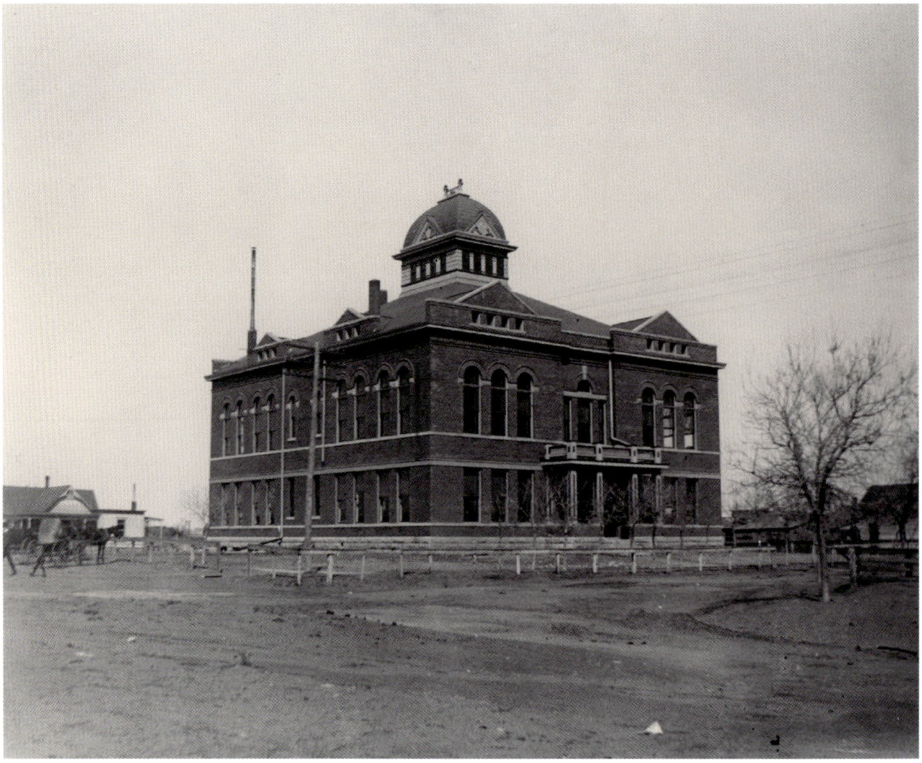

The first Woodward County courthouse (shown in 1902) was built on the corner of Tenth Street and Texas Avenue in 1901. The building faced the east (Tenth Street). The cupola was a unique feature but was later removed. The building remained county offices and courts until the new courthouse was built in 1935. It was torn down after being severely damaged in the April 1947 tornado. The location is presently the main branch of the Stock Exchange Bank of Woodward.

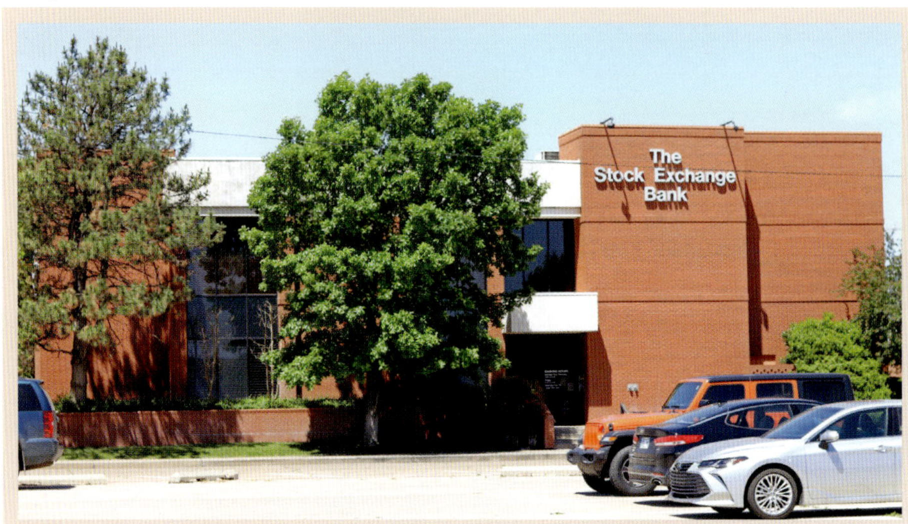

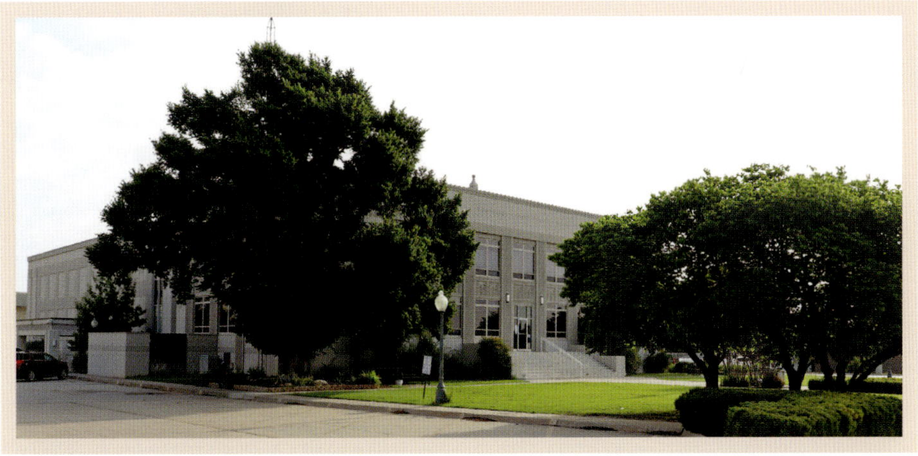

The present Woodward County Courthouse was built in 1935 at 1600 Main Street. The 1947 tornado caused extensive damage to the building, with nearly all the windows blown out and structural damage to the upper third. The photograph below shows the courthouse following the post-tornado repairs. A major construction project focused on building a new jail was undertaken in 2009.

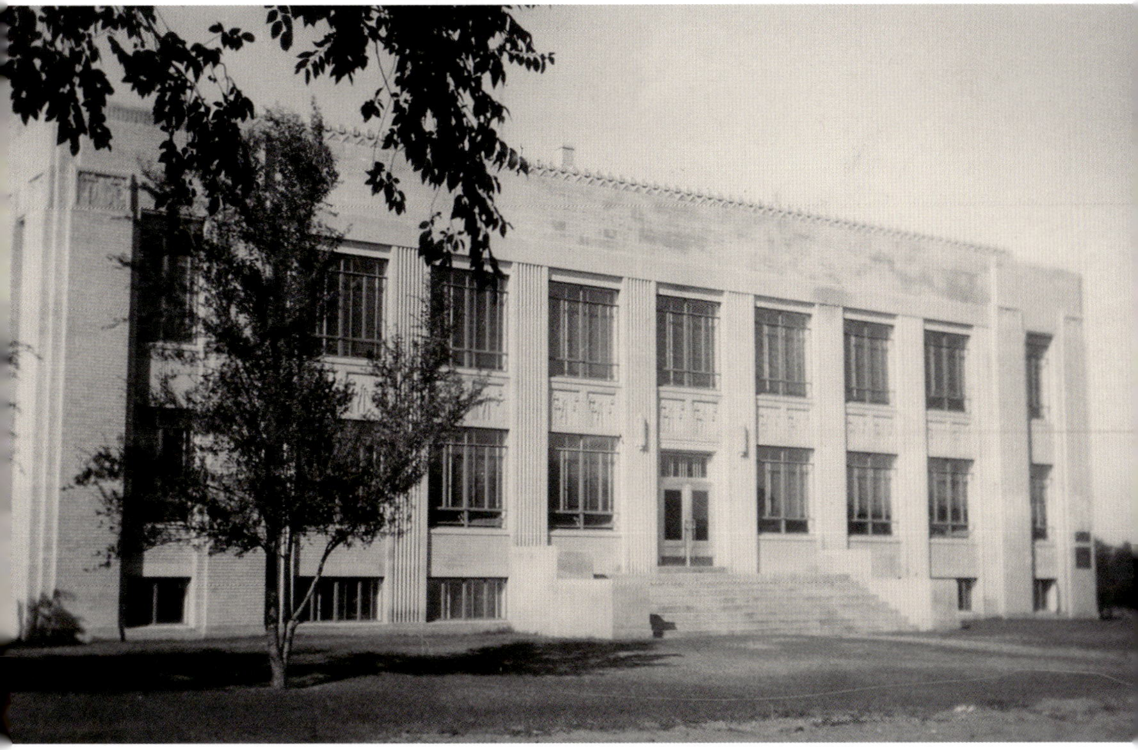

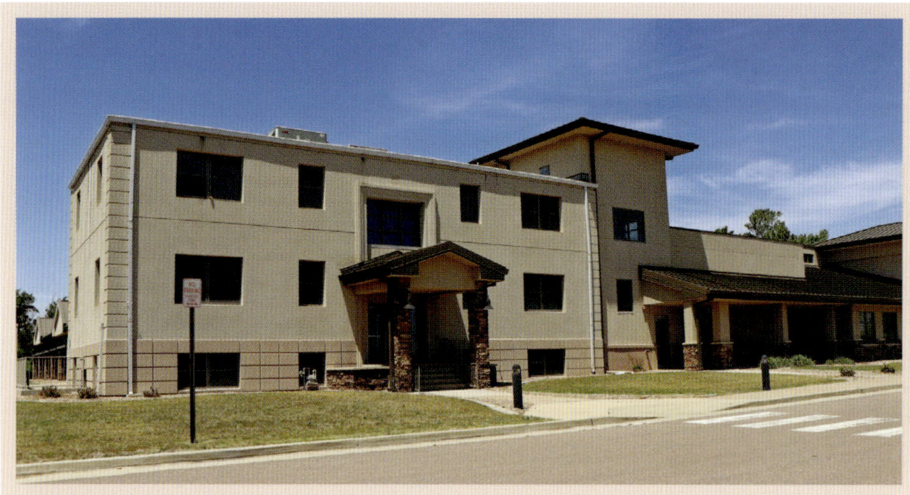

The USDA's Southern Great Plains Field Station, now known as the Southern Plains Range Research Station, has been an important part of Woodward and northwest Oklahoma since 1919. For more than a century, the station has provided important research into sustainable agricultural practices for rangeland and associated ecosystems. The headquarters and laboratory are seen below most likely in the late 1940s or early 1950s. The photograph above shows the structure today with additions.

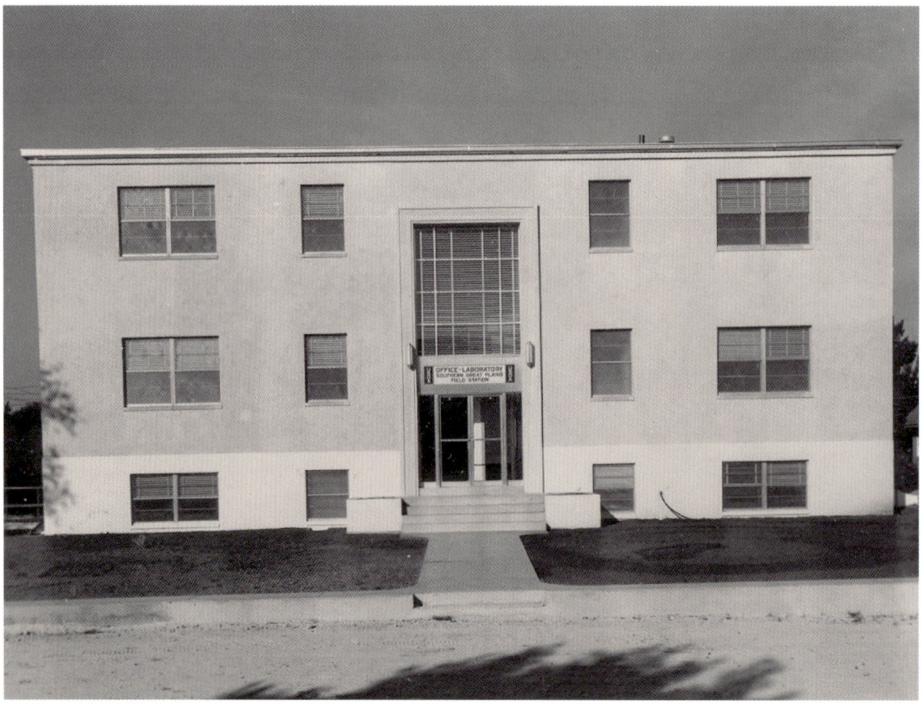

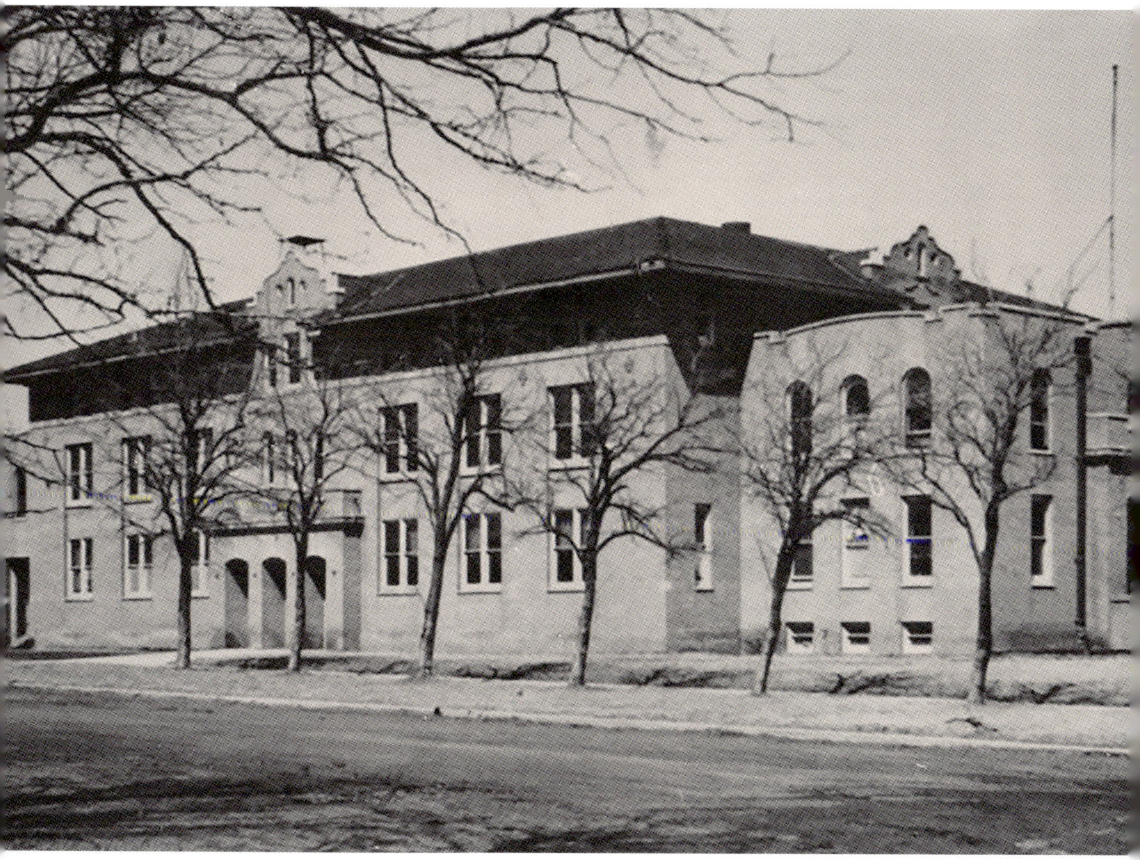

Convention Hall was built in 1917 on the northwest corner of Oklahoma Avenue and Eighth Street. It served as a venue for performing arts and conventions for most of the 20th century. Musical luminaries such as Jerry Lee Lewis and others performed there. A small city jail was on the top floor. The building served as city offices from the mid-1980s and today houses offices for the Woodward Police Department.

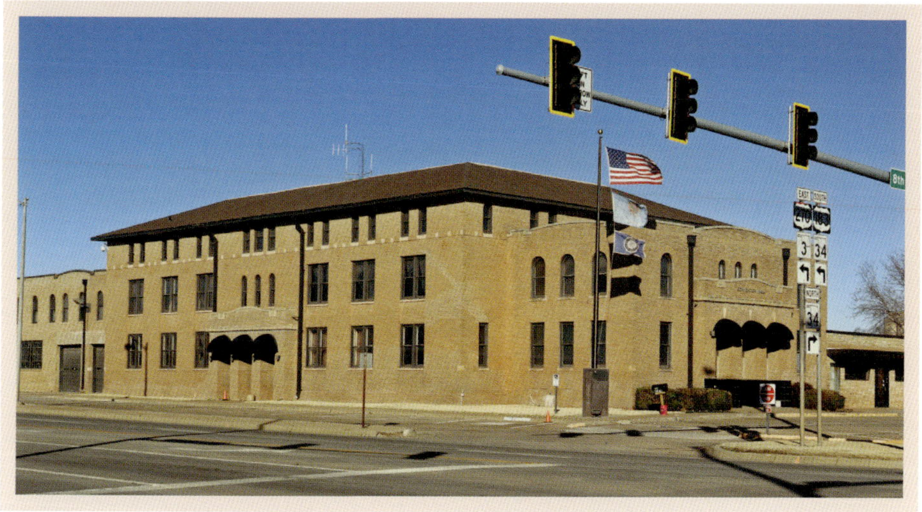

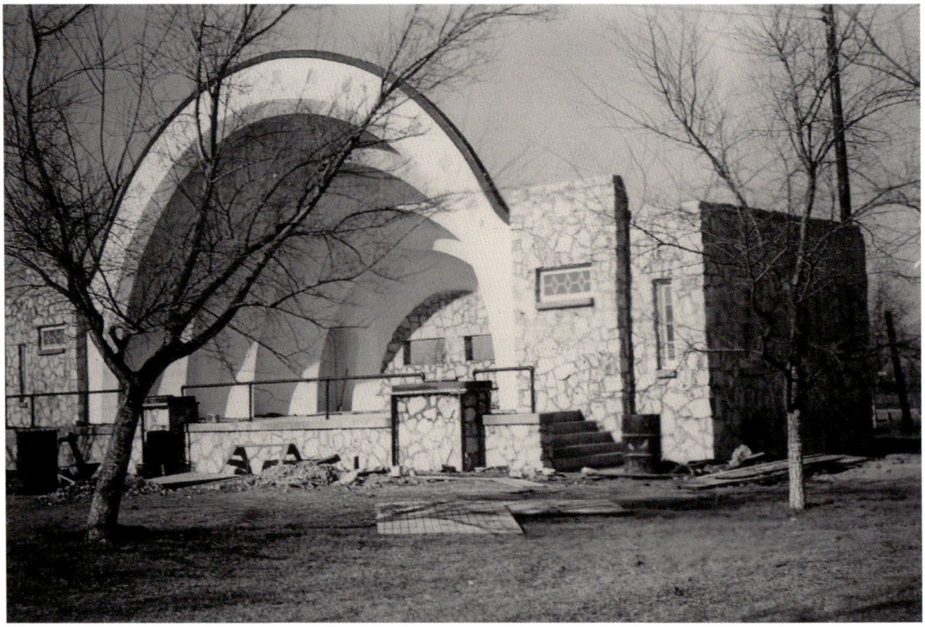

The Band Shell at Crystal Beach, administered by the City of Woodward, was completed in 1937. The amphitheater was built by the Works Progress Administration to create employment for those who lost their jobs during the Great Depression. The Band Shell is 30 feet by 70 feet and is partly constructed of flagstone. During the late 1960s and early 1970s, it was a popular venue for local bands. It rarely sees use, except during the Fourth of July celebrations and Crystal Christmas.

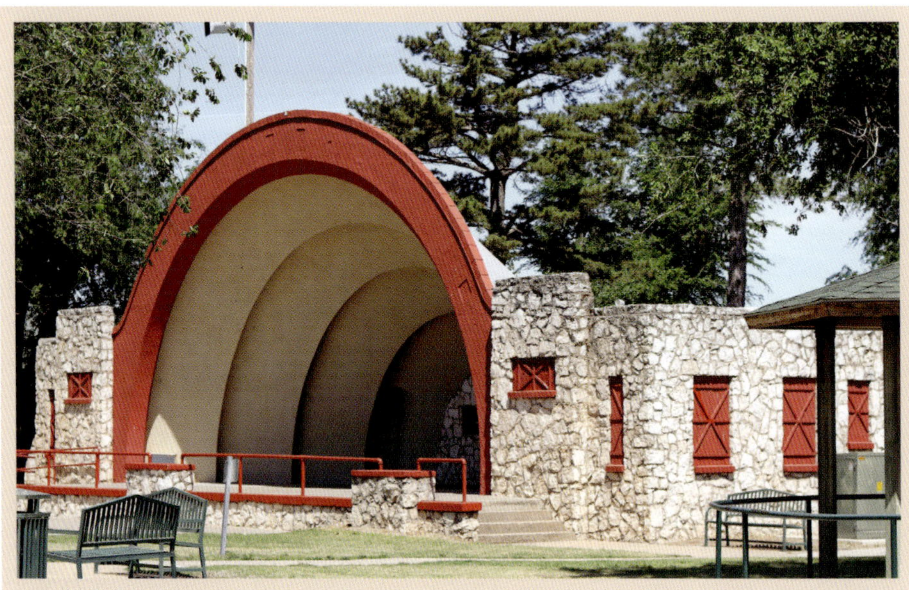

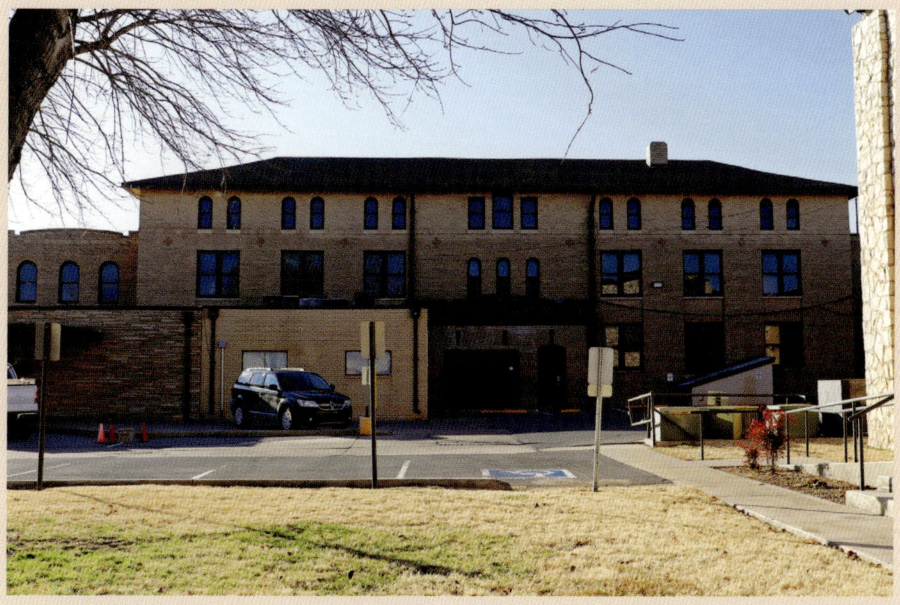

The photograph below dates to 1926 and was taken during the dedication ceremony of a Daughters of the American Revolution memorial to Woodward County veterans of World War I. The photograph above shows the site today in Centennial Park. (The old Convention Hall is in the background of both photographs.) The monument was removed by the city to the Woodward County Veterans' Memorial on Williams Avenue.

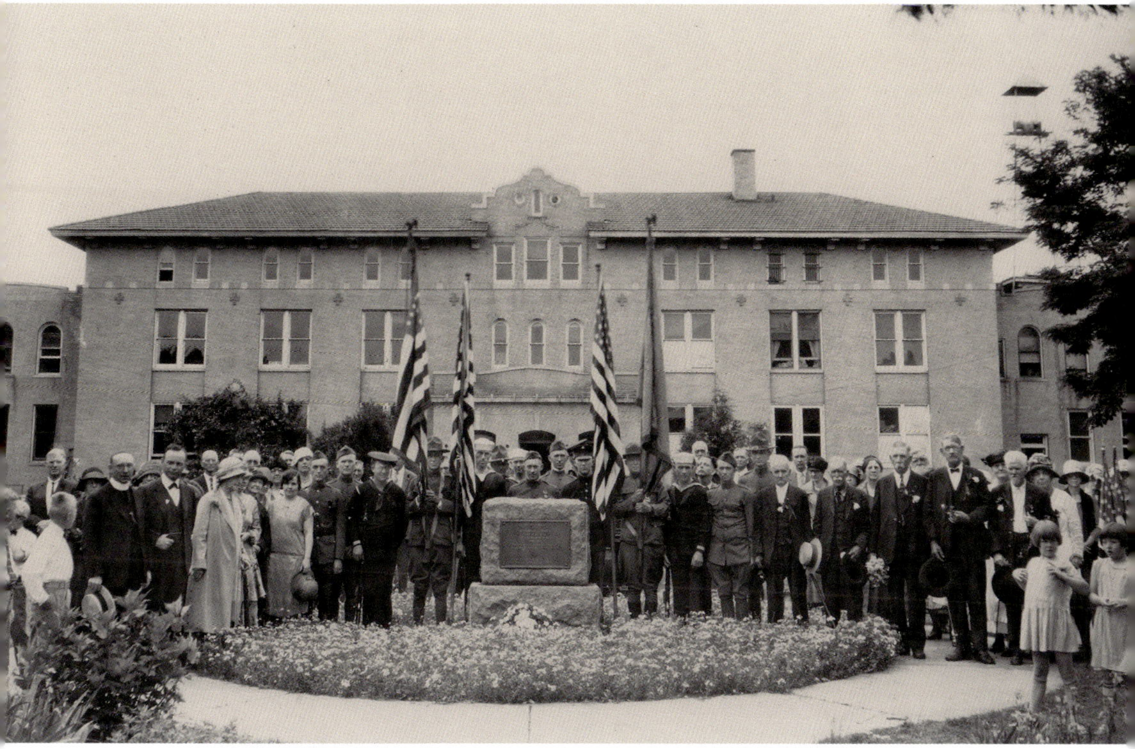

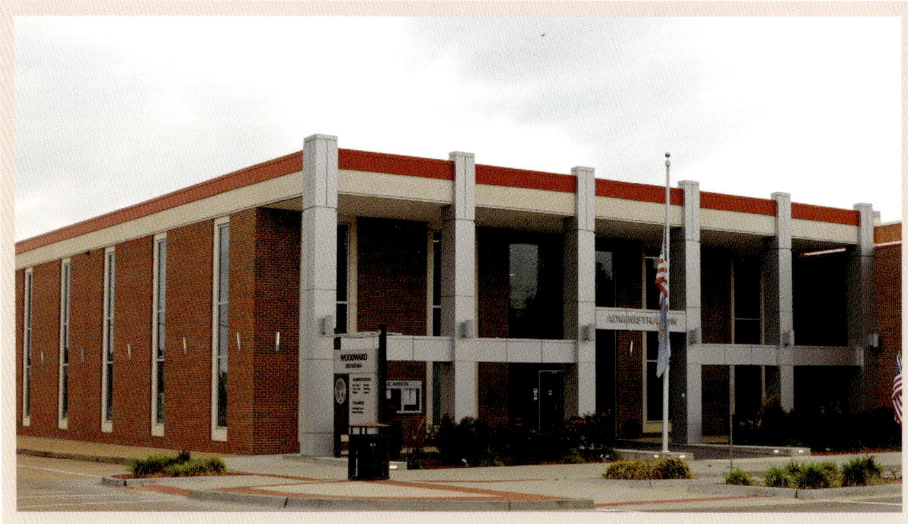

The Baker Hotel stood on the northeast corner of Eighth and Main Streets from 1912. It served as a temporary hospital and morgue following the 1947 tornado, and was demolished in the 1960s to make way for a new Bank of Woodward building. The bank building was renovated in 2016 to serve as the city's administrative offices. Note the hack parked in front of the hotel, used to transport customers from the train stations.

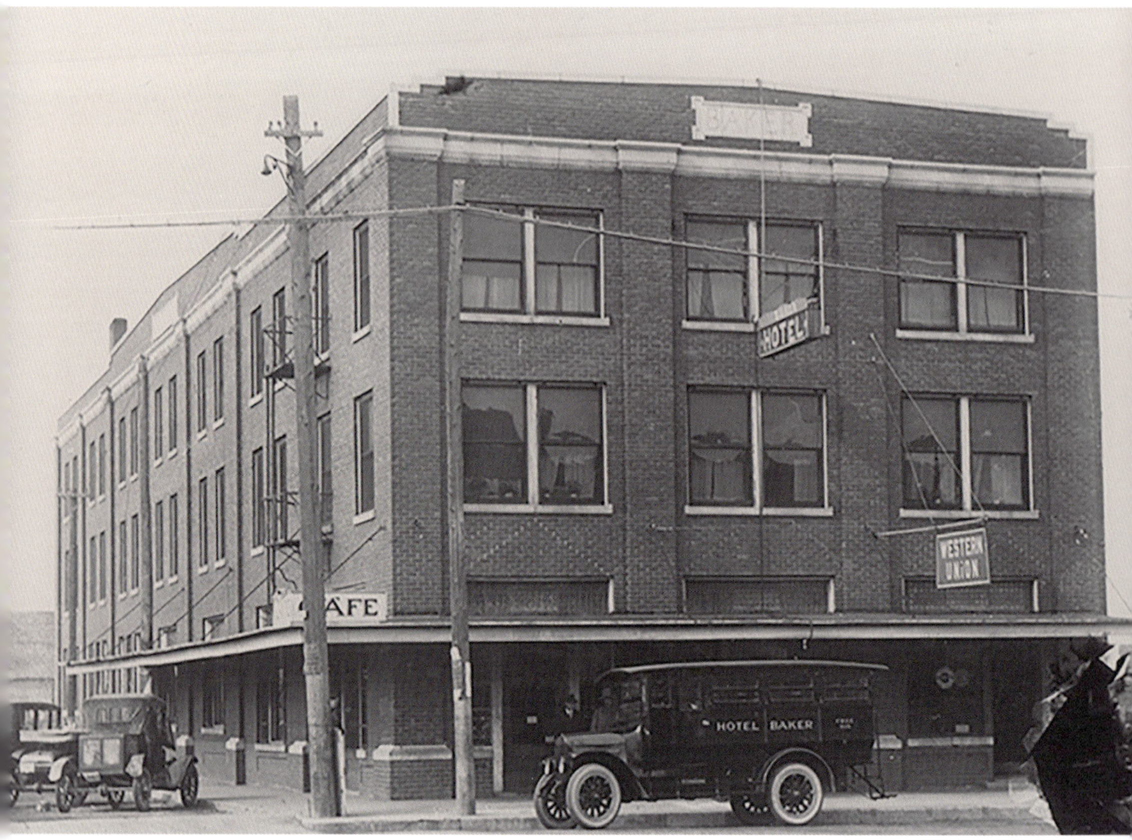

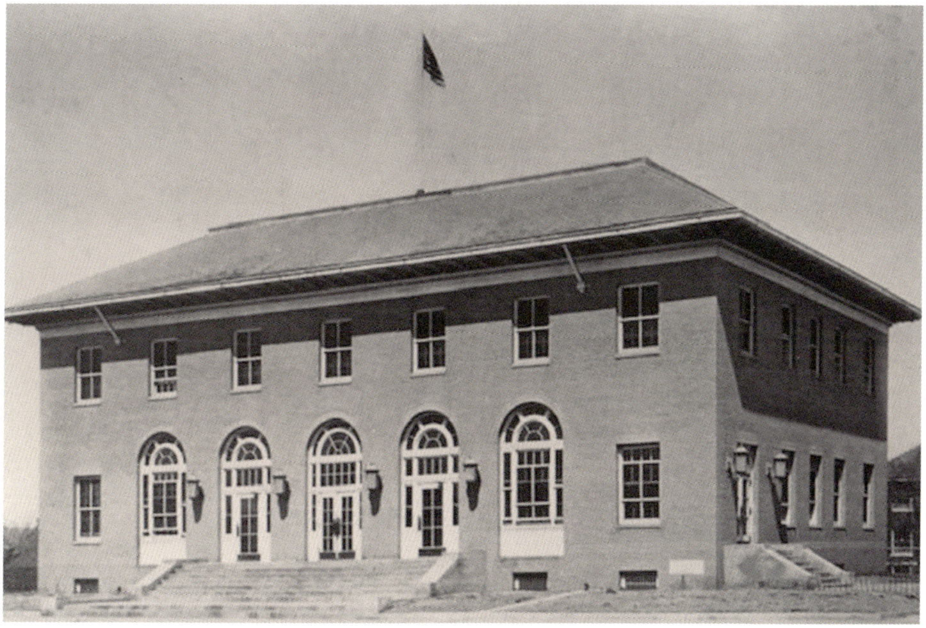

The old "Federal Building" today serves as the administrative offices of Woodward Public Schools. Prior to that, it served for decades as the US Post Office and, from its opening as a federal building, housed federal offices and even federal courts. The Woodward Public Schools have kept much of the original architecture and layout in place. Many of the windows on the second floor still hold the original glass.

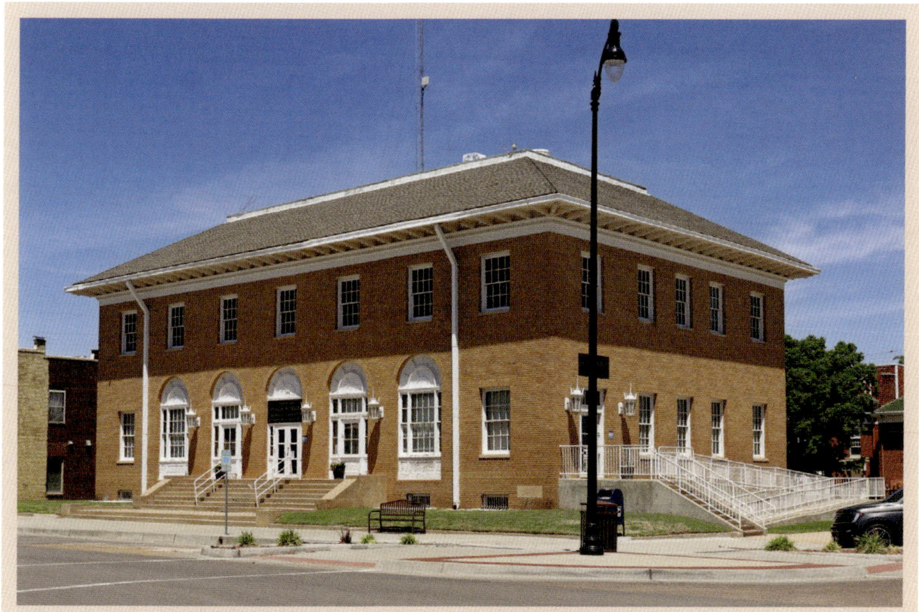

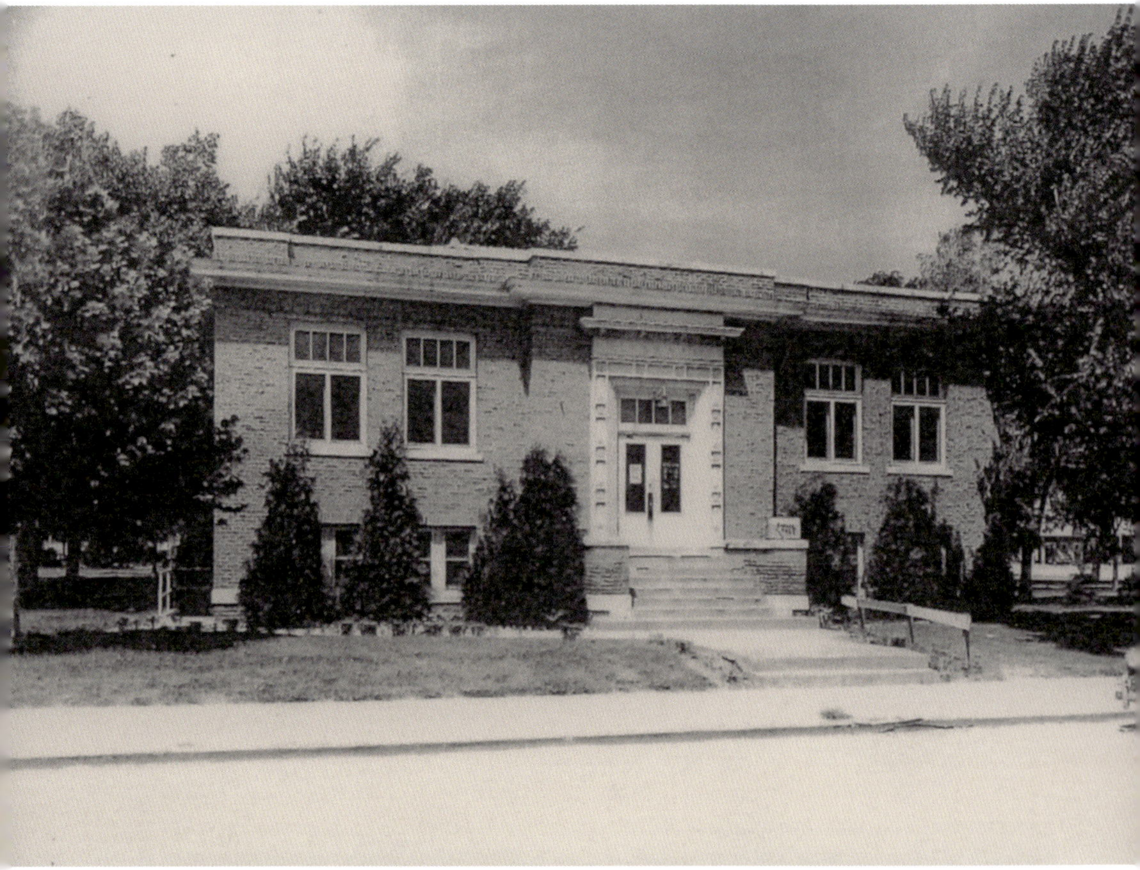

The Carnegie Library was built with a grant of $10,000 from Andrew Carnegie and opened on May 1, 1917. At the start, the library had only 450 books to lend, but by 1934, that number reached 38,016. The Woodward Public Library moved to a new location in 1988. The Carnegie building is used today by the city's facilities maintenance department. (Above, courtesy of Woodward Public Library.)

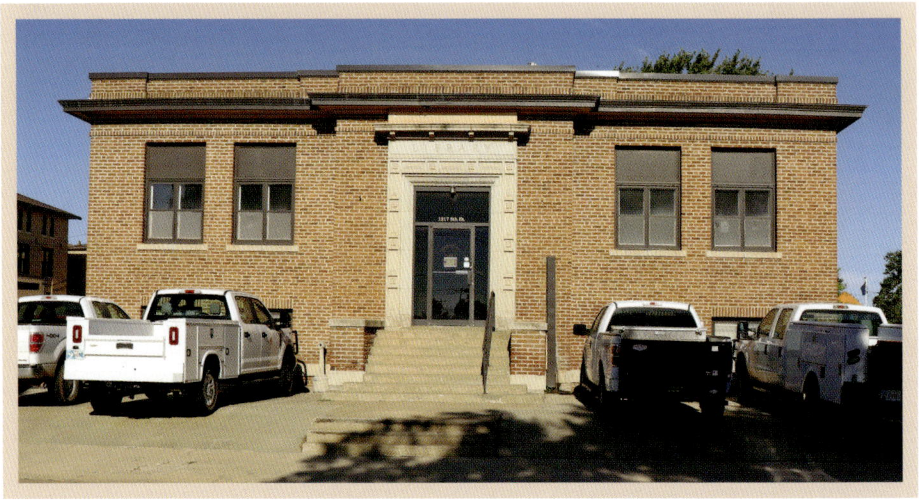

CHAPTER 3

SHELTER

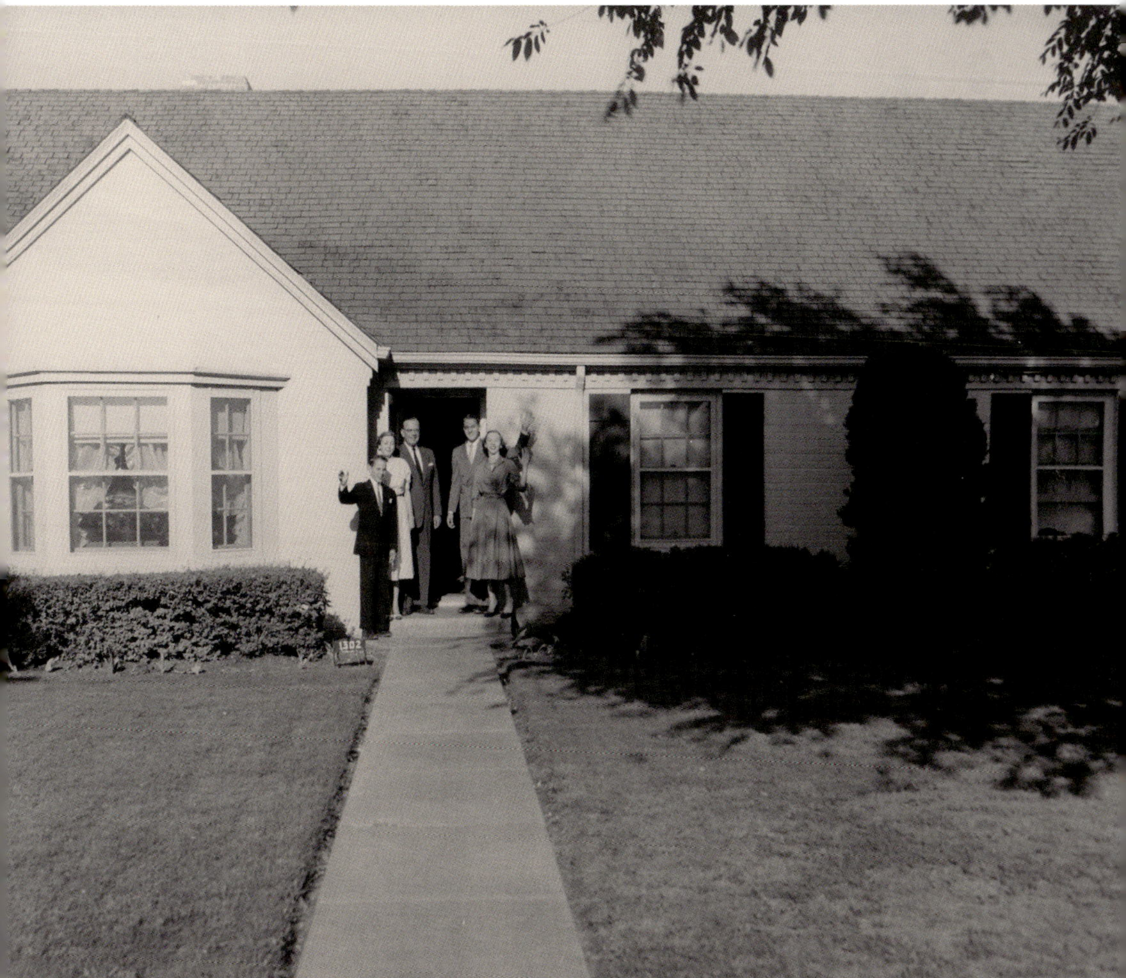

This home sits on the corner of Oklahoma Avenue and Seventeenth Street. The family waving from the front porch are the Sparks, and the photograph likely dates to the early 1960s. The house looks very different today. At some point, the paint was removed, leaving the natural red brick color.

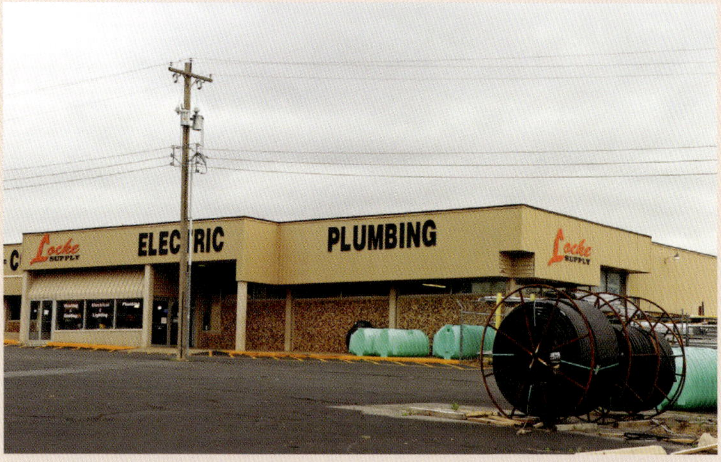

The house that Temple Houston built in 1898 sat on what was originally the far western reaches of the city at 1415 Texas Avenue. In the undated photograph below, Laura Houston is shown behind her daughter Mary, and her son Sam is holding a dog. The home remained in the Houston family until the 1970s, when it was bulldozed for construction of a grocery store. The location is today Locke Supply.

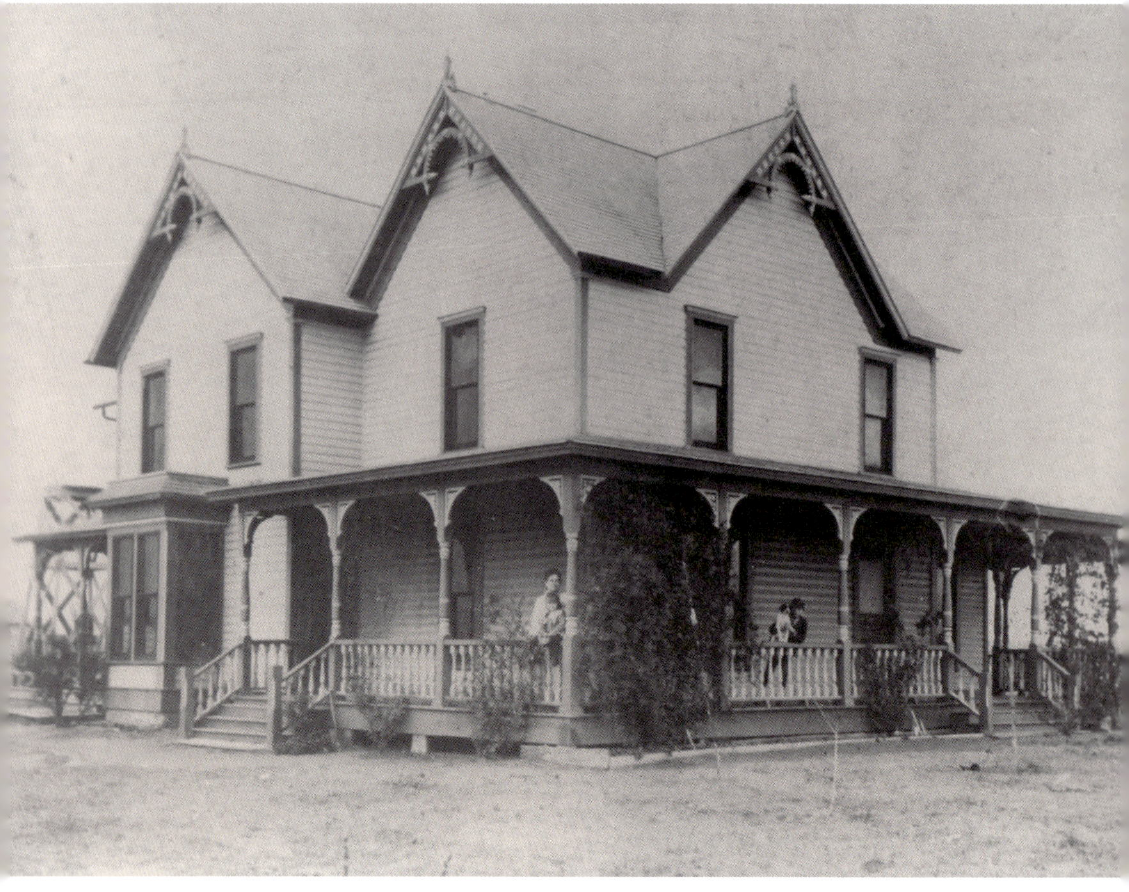

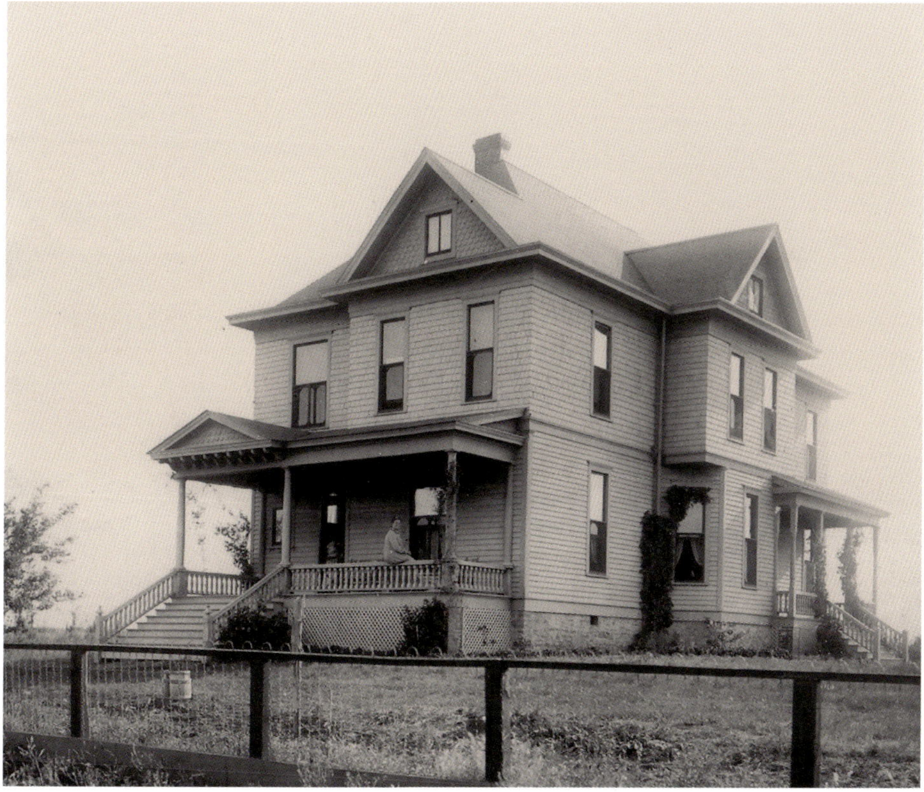

Rancher A.H. Tandy built this magnificent home in 1899 on the corner of what is now Fourteenth Street and Oklahoma Avenue. The original home had 14 rooms, including two kitchens, a formal living room, and a library. A jail cell was set up in the basement to accommodate unruly cowboys. The home was razed in the late 1970s for the construction of a fast-food restaurant. Today it is the site of the Jewelry Station retail store.

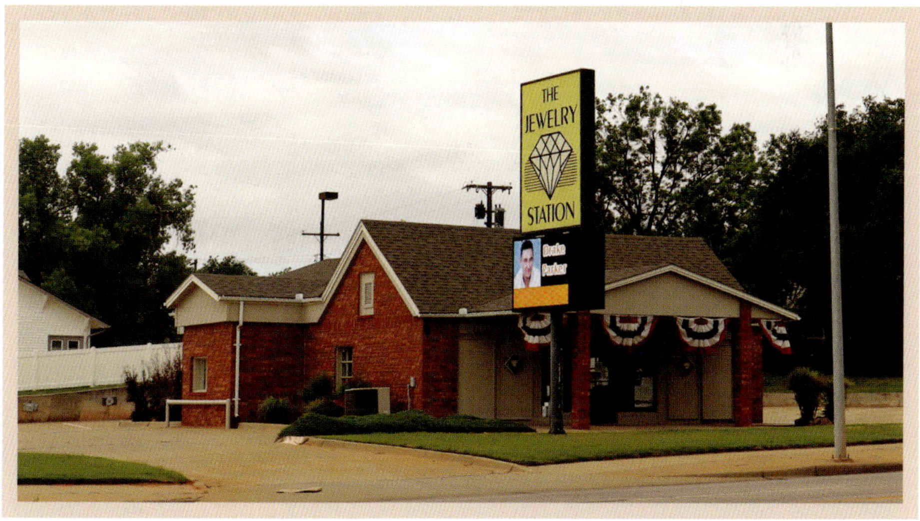

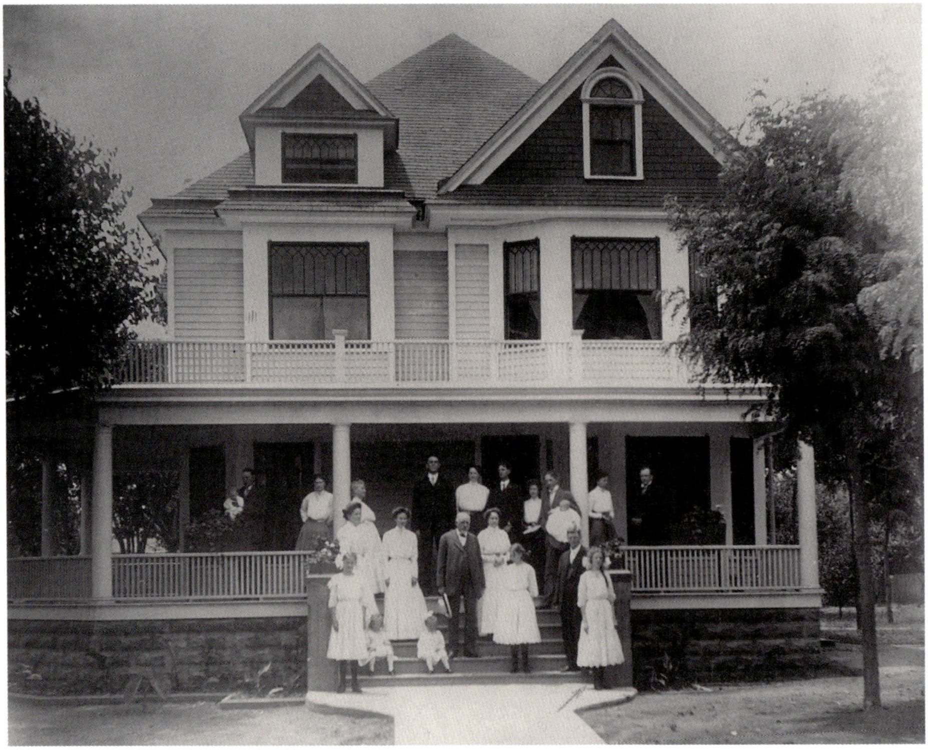

The above photograph of the John Gerlach home dates to 1909. The people on the porch were gathered for a wedding. Gerlach was a respected banker and businessman with ties to Woodward from the 1890s. The three-story home later became the location of the SW Bell Telephone company offices and now serves as a location for AT&T services in the city.

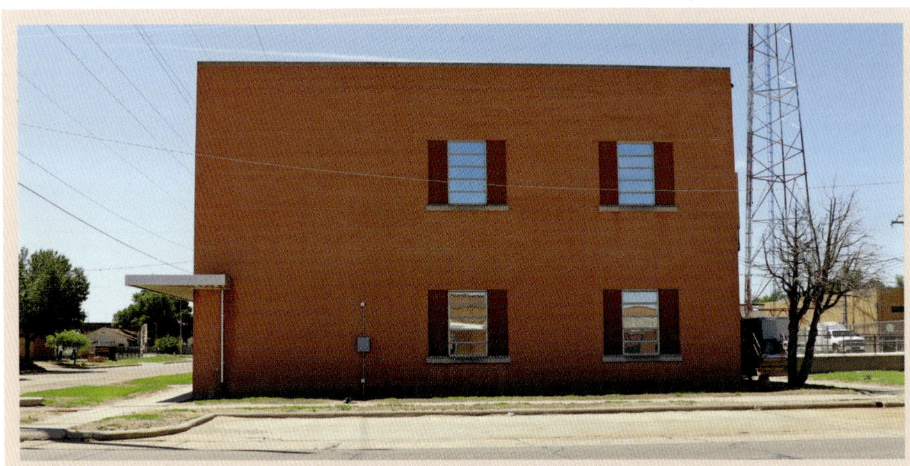

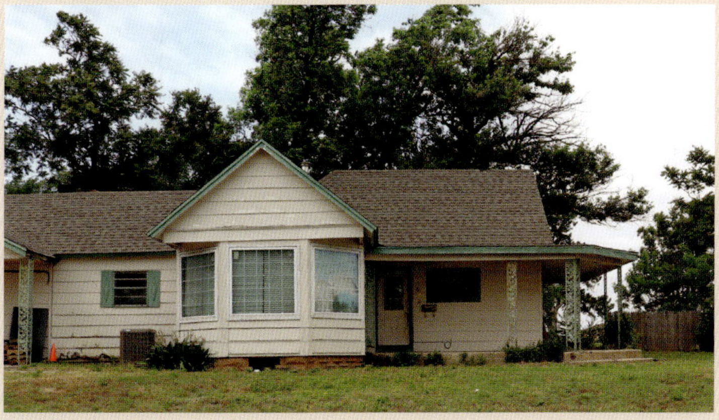

The photograph below was taken in June 1913 on the occasion of the marriage of Connie Beatte to L.T. Sanders. The wedding party is on the front porch of the Beatte home. The bride is in the hat on the lawn at left center. Standing to her right is the groom. The Beattes were prominent pioneers in Woodward. The house remains on the southwest corner of Sixth Street and Oklahoma Avenue.

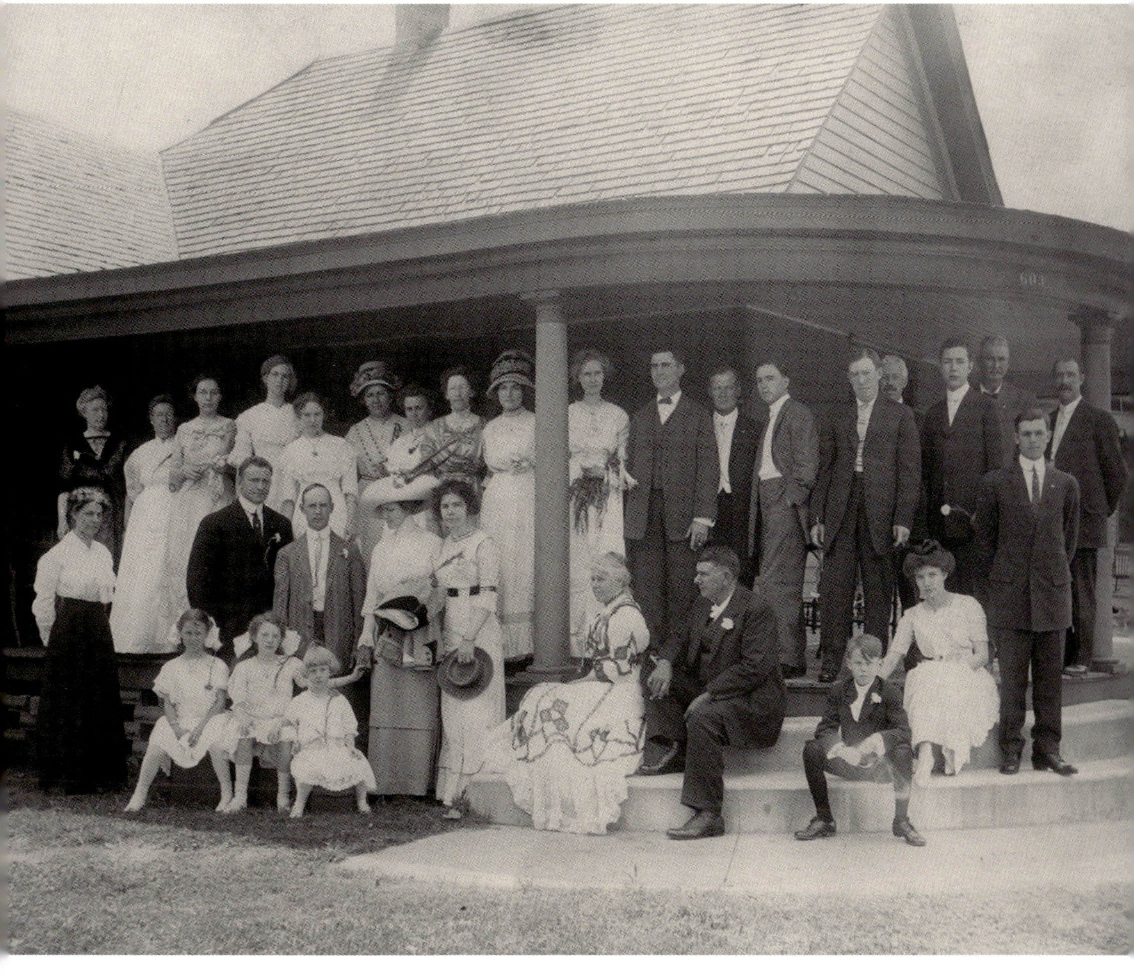

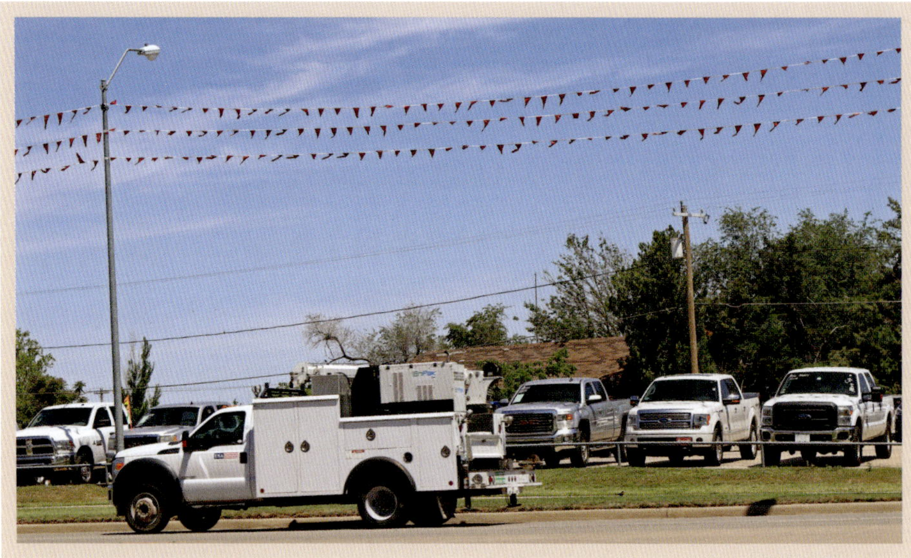

This magnificent example of a type of home usually found in the deep South was known as the Thompson House. It was near the northeast corner of Sixth Street and Oklahoma Avenue. In the 1990s, during construction to widen Oklahoma Avenue, the home was moved south of Mooreland, Oklahoma. Today, the site is the far west end of the Woodward Auto-Mart dealership.

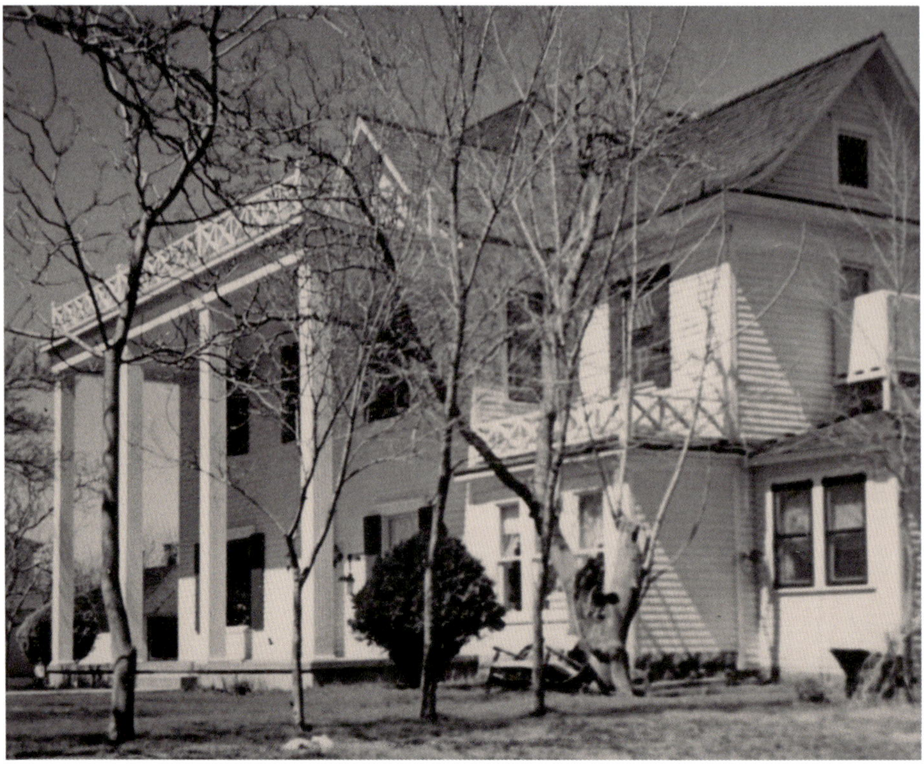

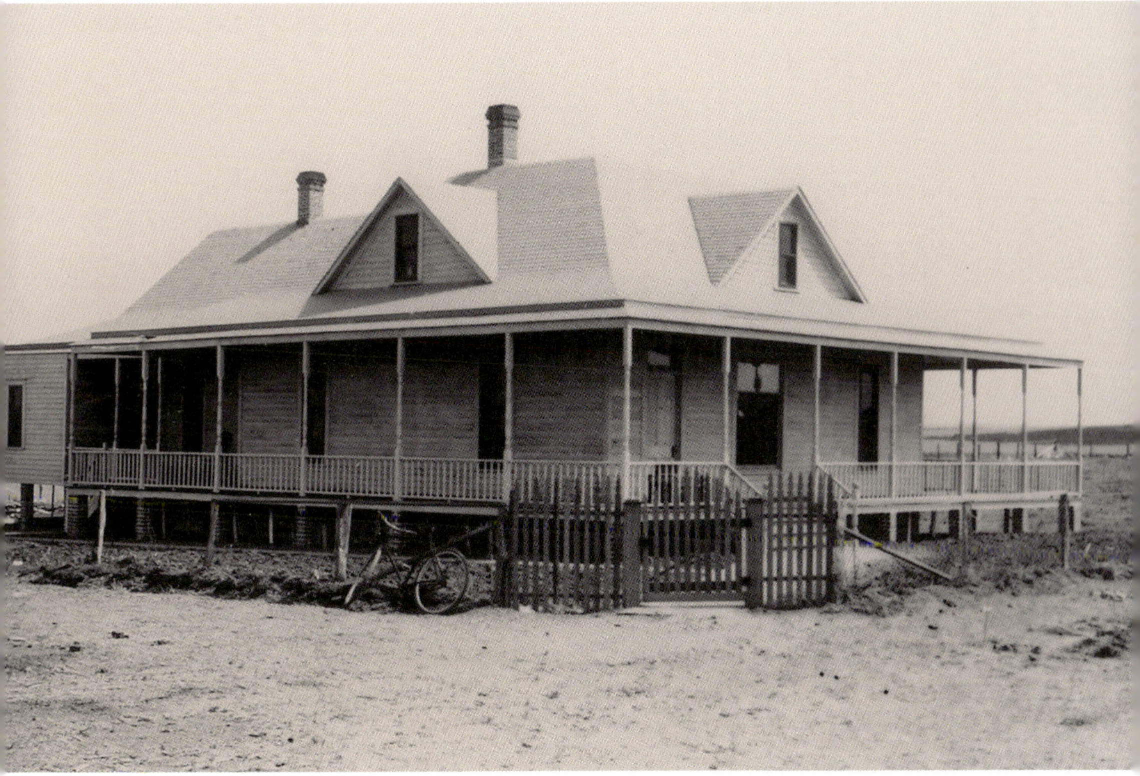

This photograph from 1905 shows a house that Ed Boyle built with a pier foundation that he said was to provide shade for his "pups and chickens," along with the skunks and snakes. Note the chicken wire fence used to keep the comfortably shaded critters close to home. The location is 1600 Eighth Street, which today puts it in the vicinity of Eighth Street and Oak Avenue.

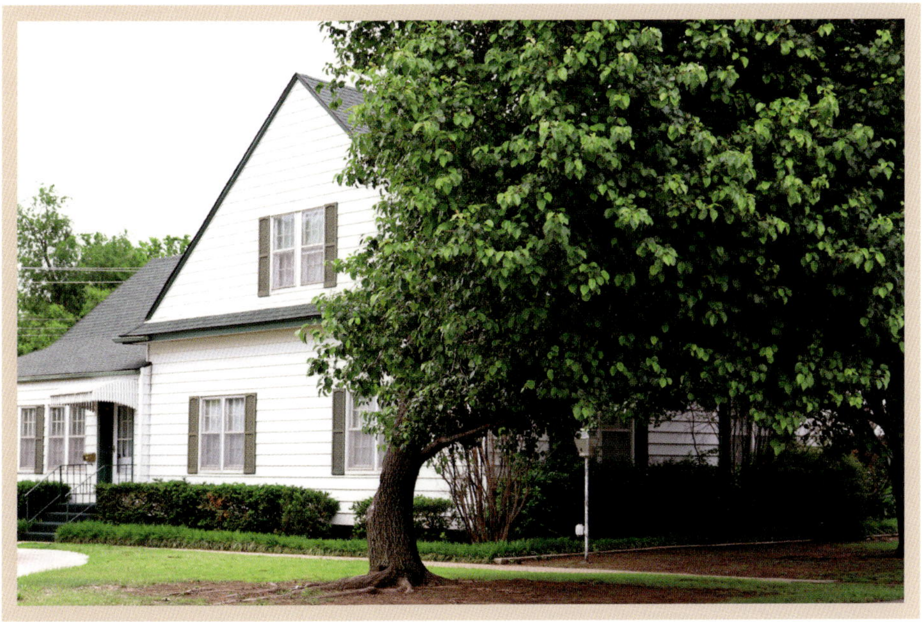

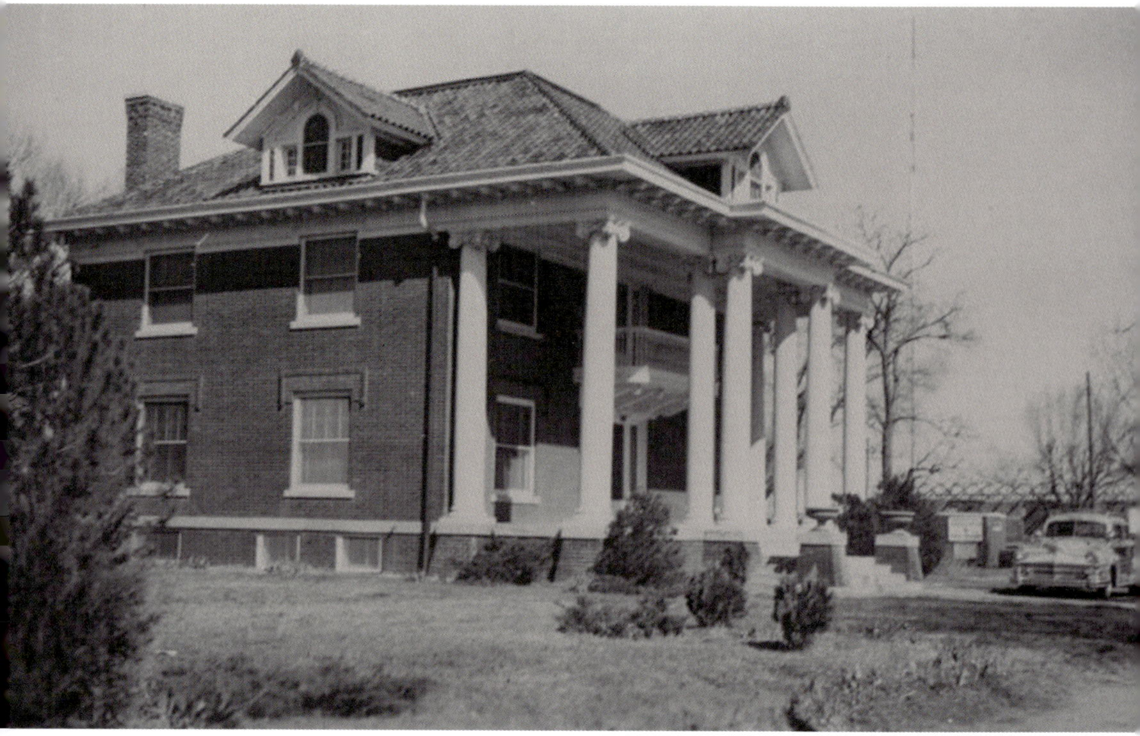

The Stine-Bradbury House was originally built by banker Len Stine in 1916 on the corner of Tenth Street and Kansas Avenue. The home was also occupied by the Harold Bradbury family, who made some significant modern improvements. This iconic Woodward mansion has stood the test of time despite suffering minor roof damage during the 1947 tornado. It is unoccupied today.

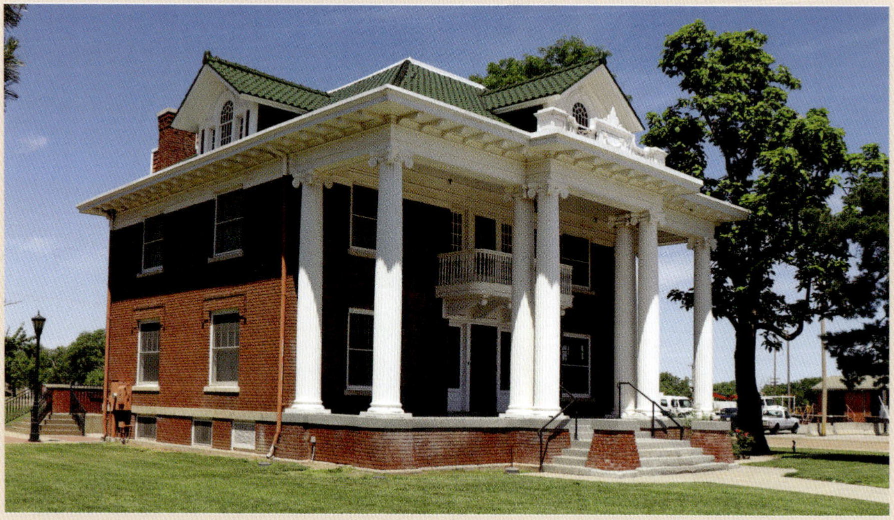

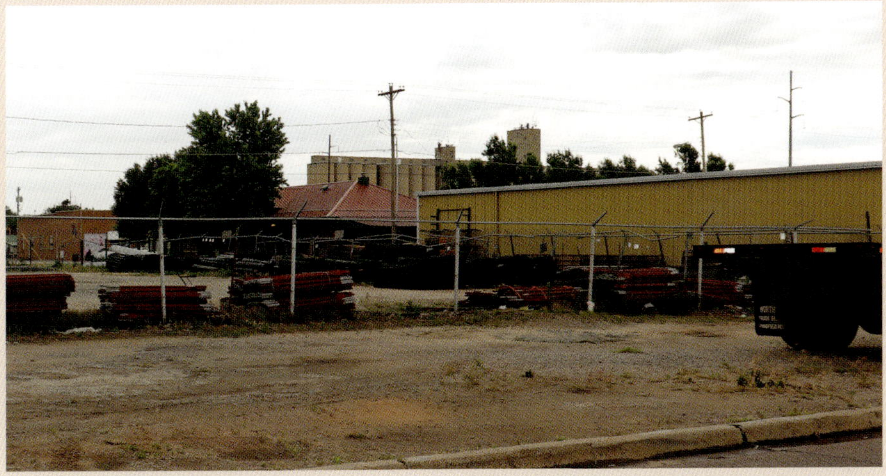

The Lidge Roberts home is seen below, at 1202 Texas Avenue. The home was a two-story structure with a large porch and plenty of shade in front. Note the front-facing gable and the dormer window. Both features were fairly common in homes built in the late 1800s and early 1900s. The photograph dates to around 1900. The location today is a storage lot for the Woodward Ace Home Center on Oklahoma Avenue.

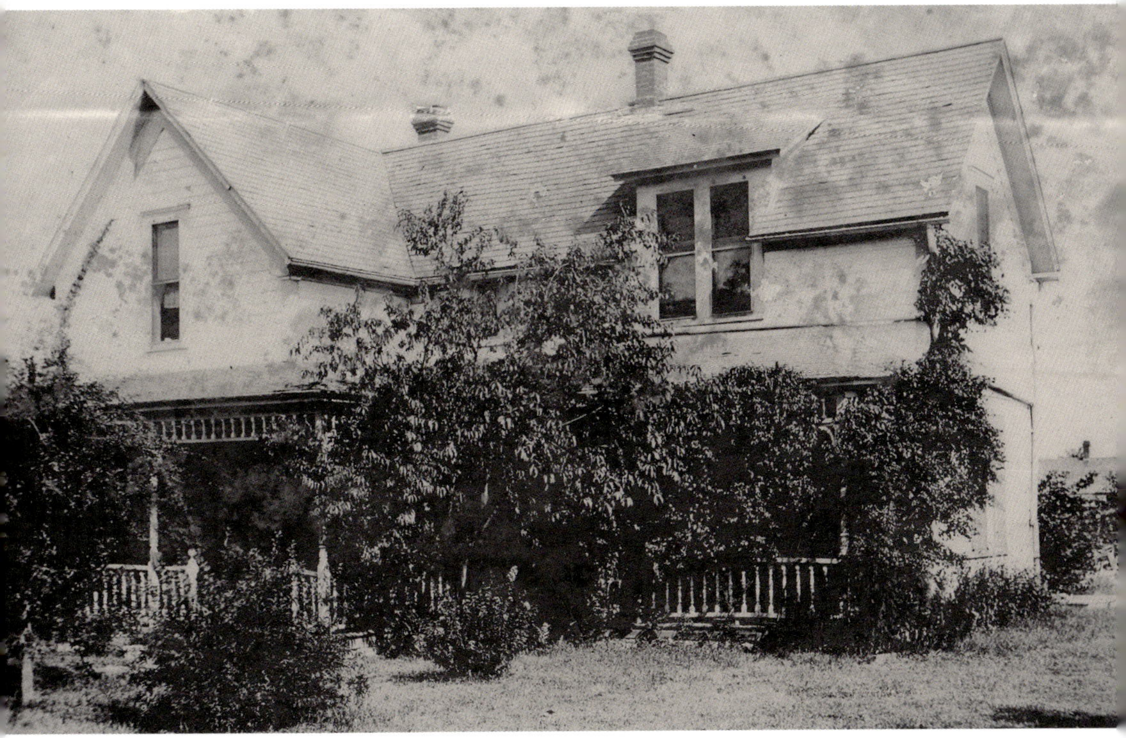

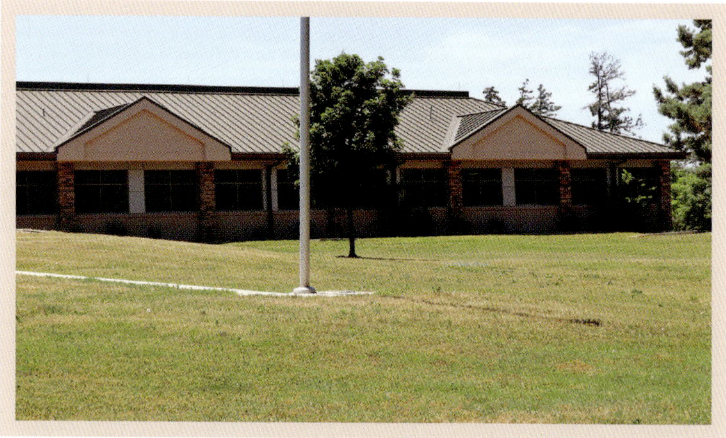

The photograph below of senior-staff housing at the Southern Great Plains Field Station was taken in 1935. The house sat just northwest of the original headquarters and laboratory building. It was torn down to make way for the addition to the new headquarters building when the field station became the Southern Plains Range Research Station.

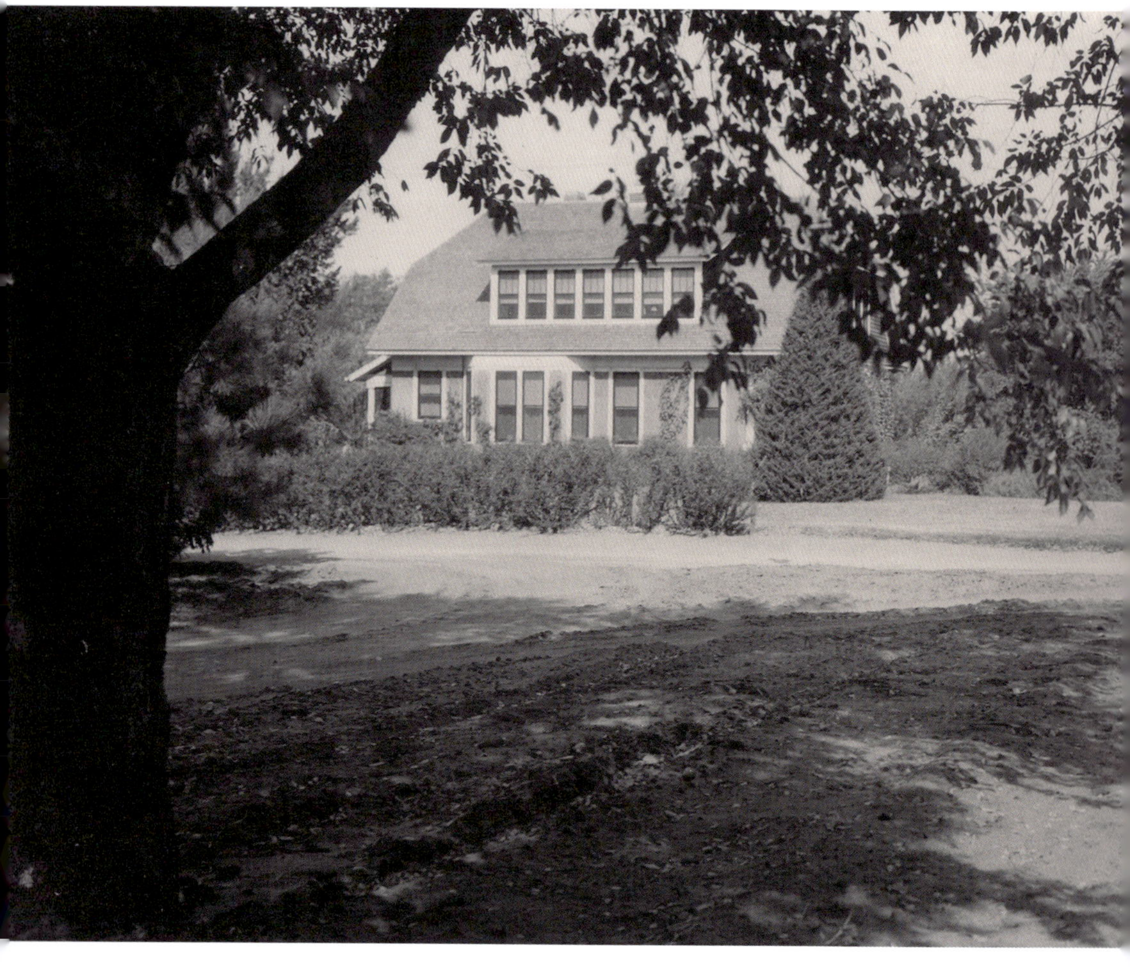

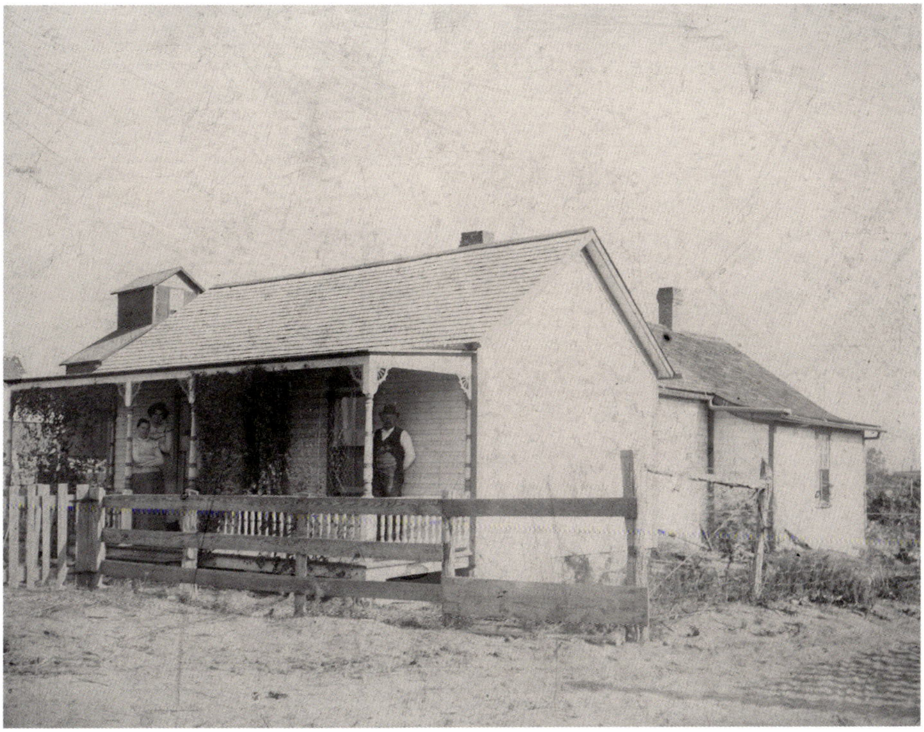

This photograph of the Peter Martinson residence along Eighth Street, just north of the Baker Hotel, was taken in the early 1900s. The three people on the porch are Peter Martinson, Tacy Martinson, and Ethel Simmons Cadwalder. Cadwalder was a family friend who lived with the Martinsons. Peter owned the Martinson General Merchandise building in the 800 block of Main Street, presently the location of Long Shots.

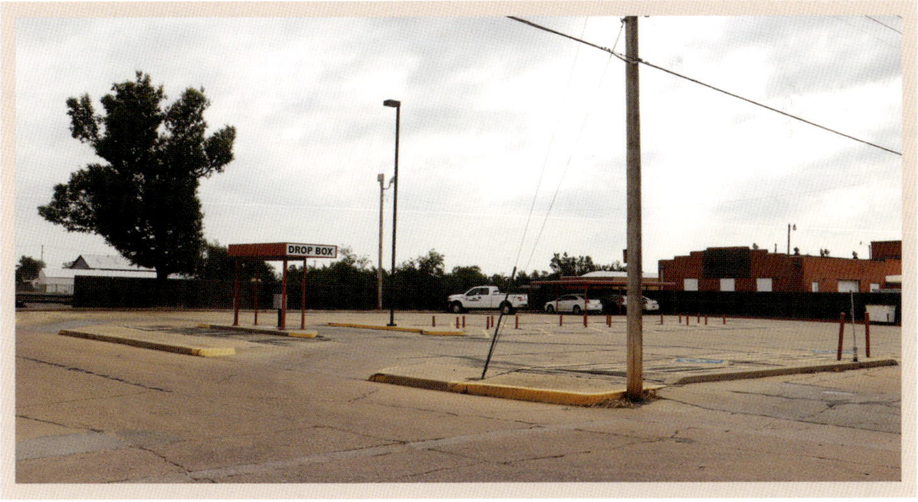

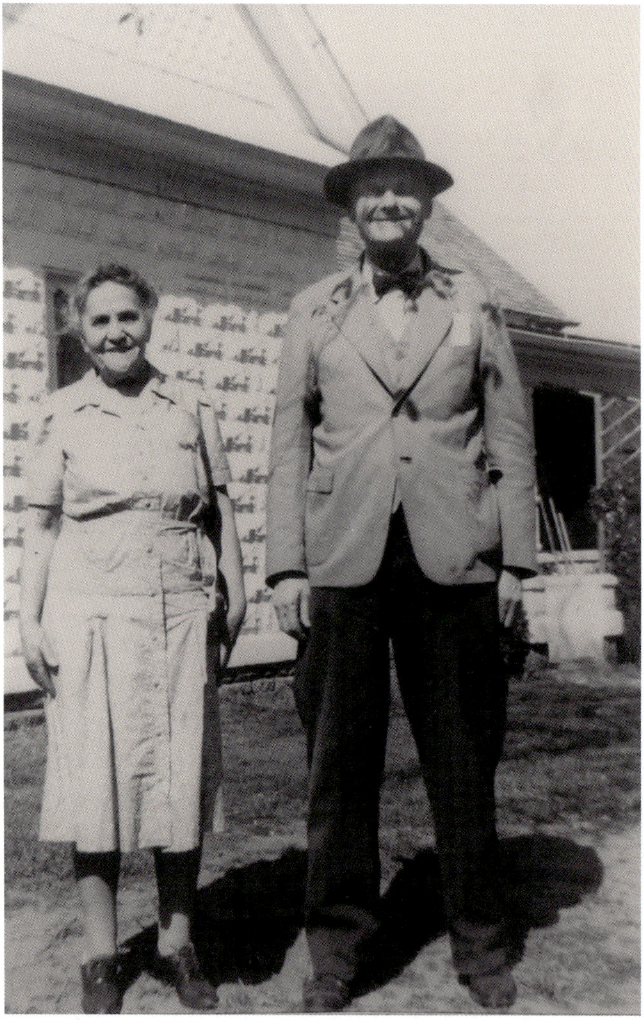

The photograph at left shows Henry and Minnie Boehm in front of their home at 1422 Third Street. They purchased the house in 1908. Henry Boehm owned Boehm's Meat Market on Main Street, which later was used as a retail store and today houses the Josie Adams Cultural Center, part of the Woodward Arts Theatre Complex. Boehm also owned a feedlot and slaughterhouse just north of Woodward along Ninth Street, on the north side of the Canadian River.

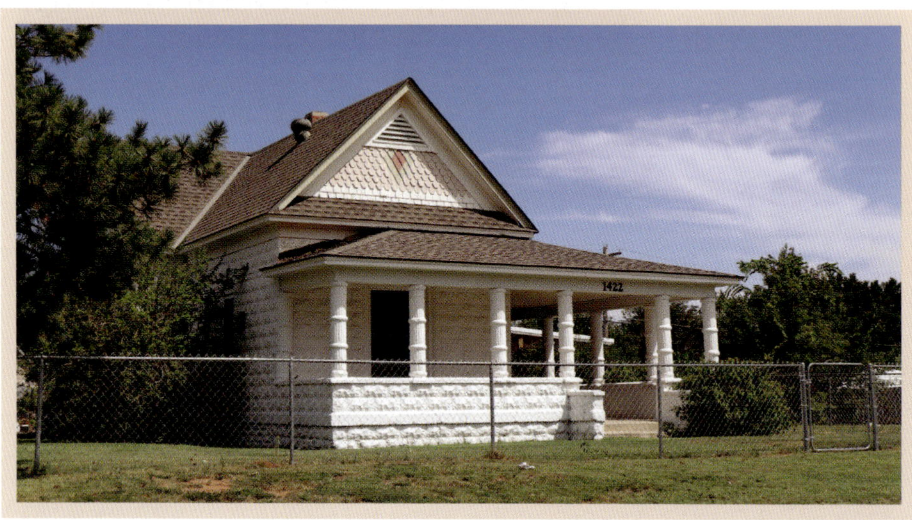

CHAPTER 4

WORSHIP

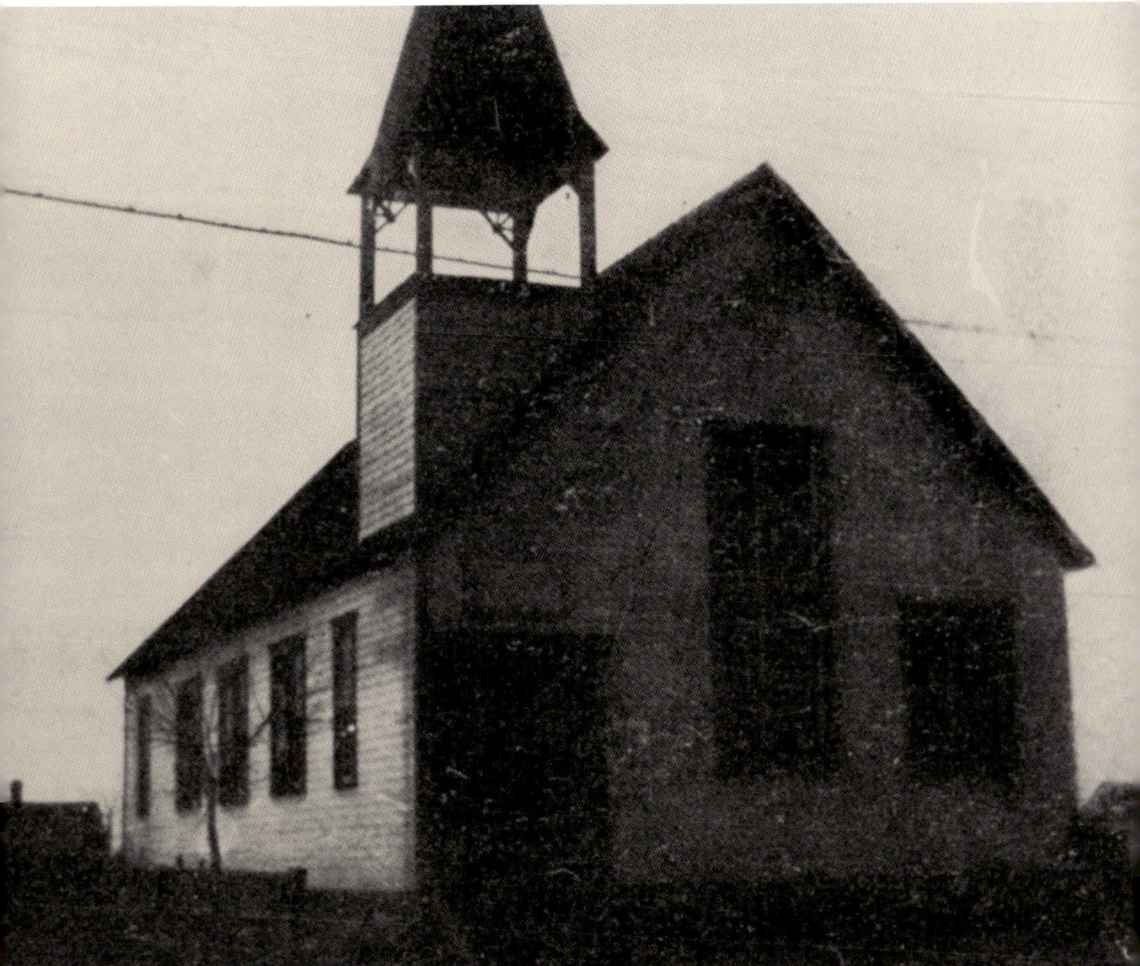

The original Christian Church of Woodward was built in 1904 on a corner lot purchased for $350 at Eleventh and Main Streets. The church was organized by R.S. Smedley, evangelist of the Oklahoma Territory Missionary Board, on September 26, 1902.

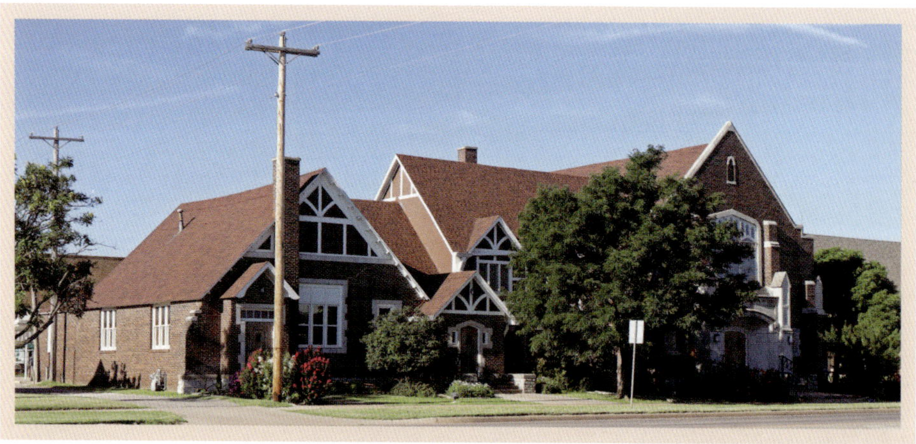

When the First Presbyterian Church of Woodward was formed in 1899, it met in a variety of homes and temporary locations; it was not until 1929 that the church, as it exists today at the corner of Eighth Street and Oklahoma Avenue, was dedicated in a formal ceremony. The church purchased a used pipe organ from a Presbyterian church in Enid and had it installed in the newly constructed building. In the 1957 photograph below, Oklahoma Avenue is unpaved.

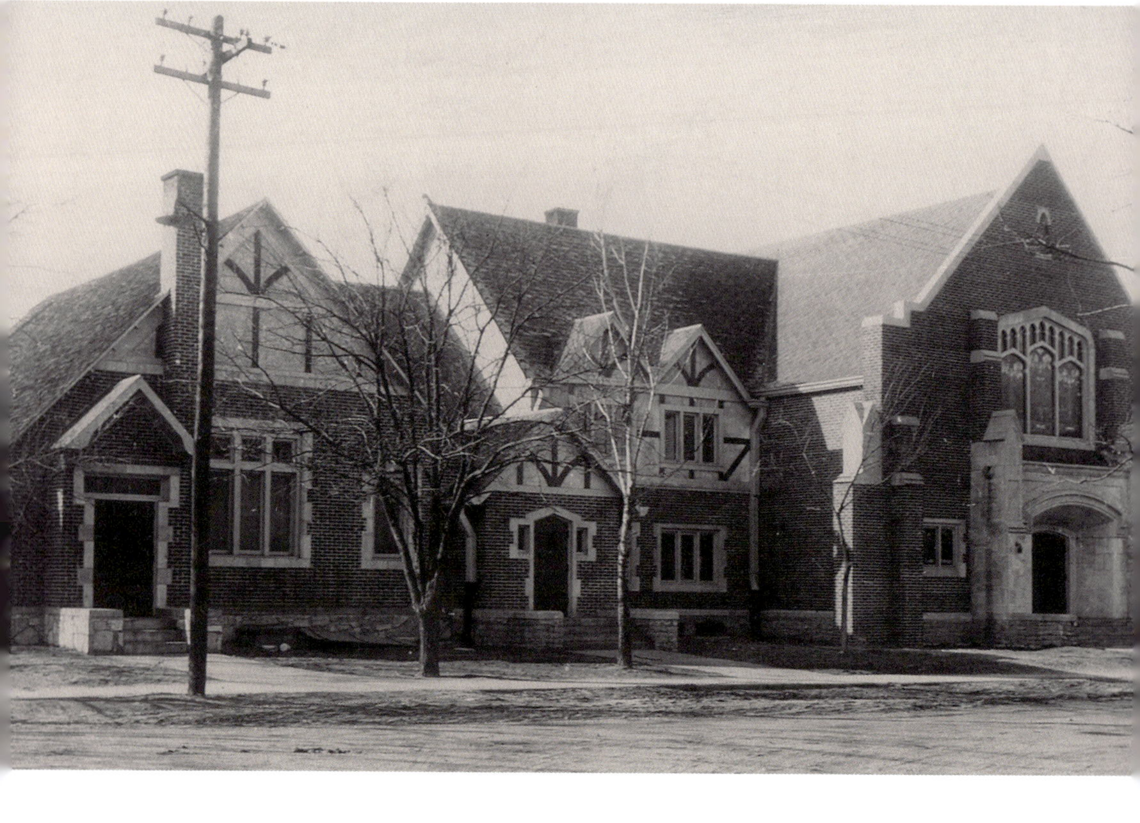

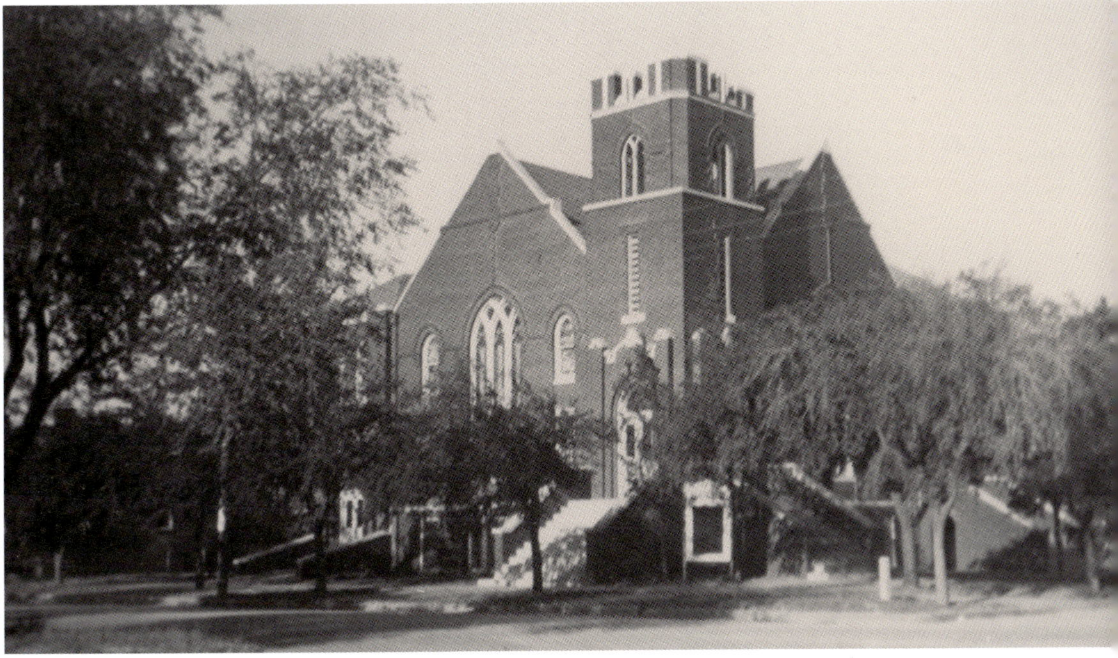

Woodward's First Baptist Church was originally constructed on the corner of Tenth Street and Oklahoma Avenue in 1917. By 1958, with the congregation growing from 300 to more than 1,200, a major construction project was undertaken to expand it to the east and north. The building was demolished in the early 1980s, and the church moved to a new building on Hanks Trail. The building on the site today houses an insurance company and several professional services.

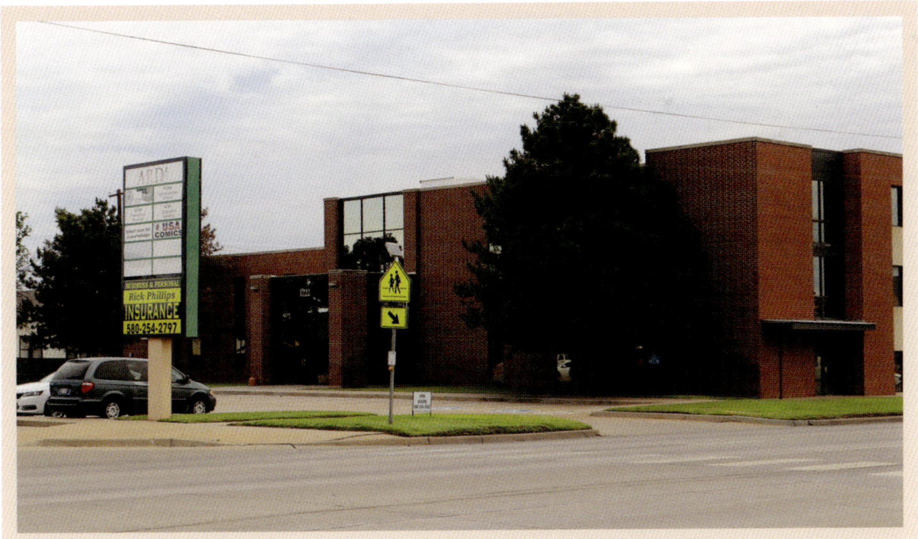

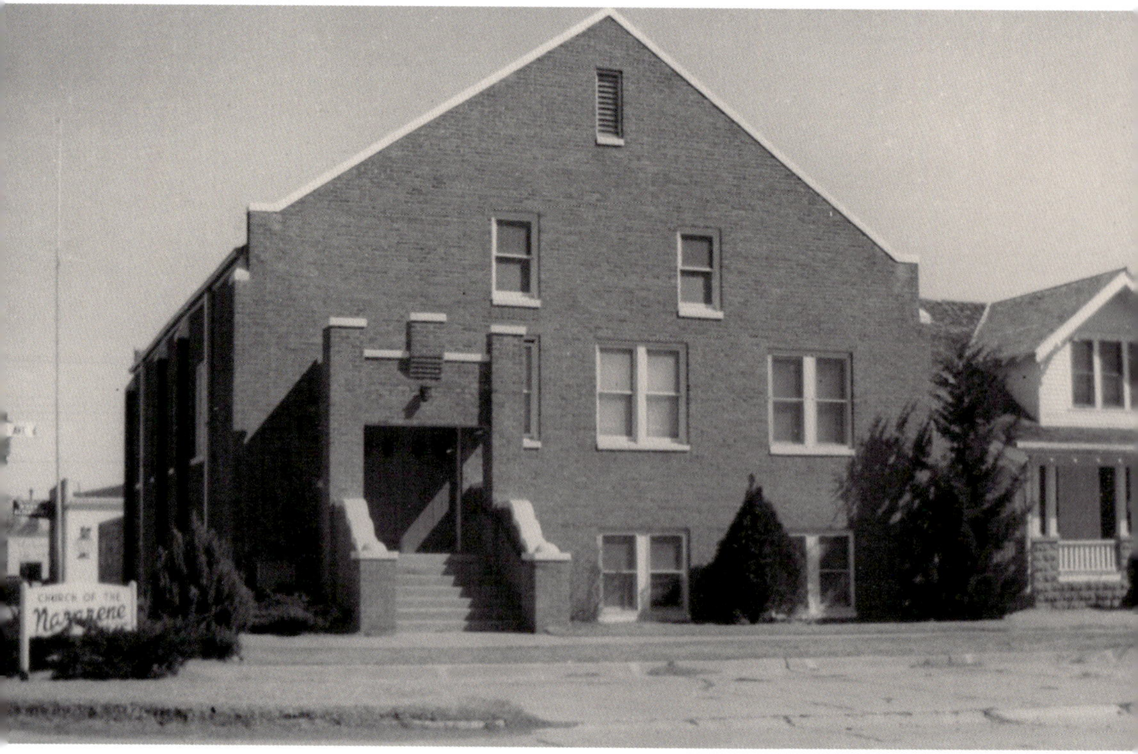

The original Woodward Church of the Nazarene was built in 1916 on the corner of Fifth Street and Texas Avenue. When the church hosted its 50th anniversary, a newspaper article about the celebration stated that it would include a dedication ceremony for recent improvements and that there were no charter members still living. The congregation moved to a new location on Downs Avenue in 1980. The Fifth Street Building is currently in use by the Sure Foundation Church of God.

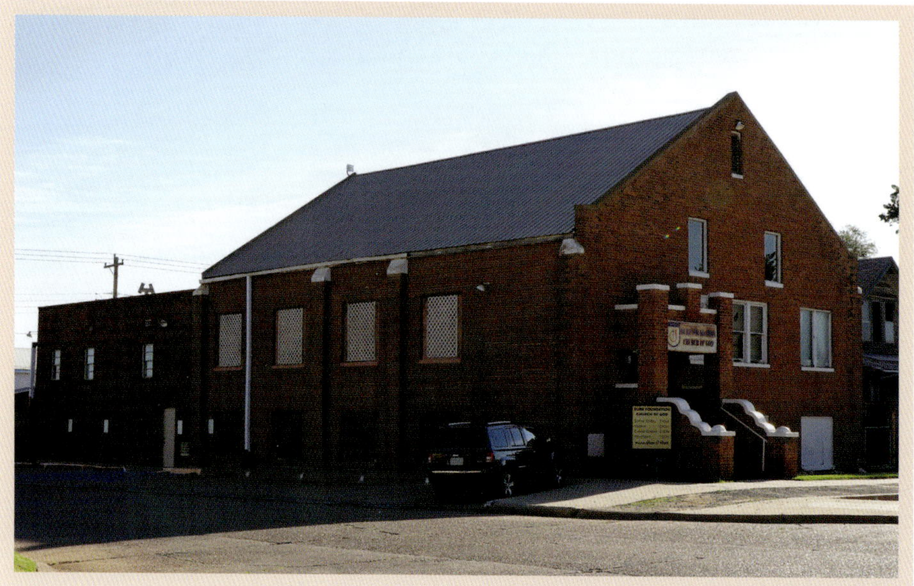

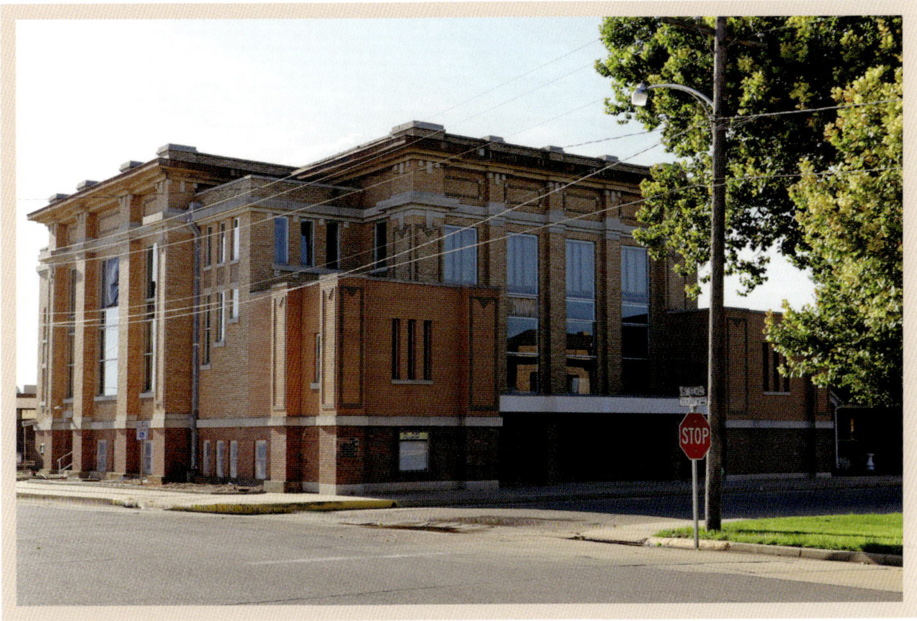

The First United Methodist Church, as it appears below, was built in the 1920s on the corner of Eighth Street and Texas Avenue. A major renovation was undertaken in 1969, as shown above. The building was sold when the congregation moved into a new church on Downs Avenue. The building is currently used by His Place Fellowship.

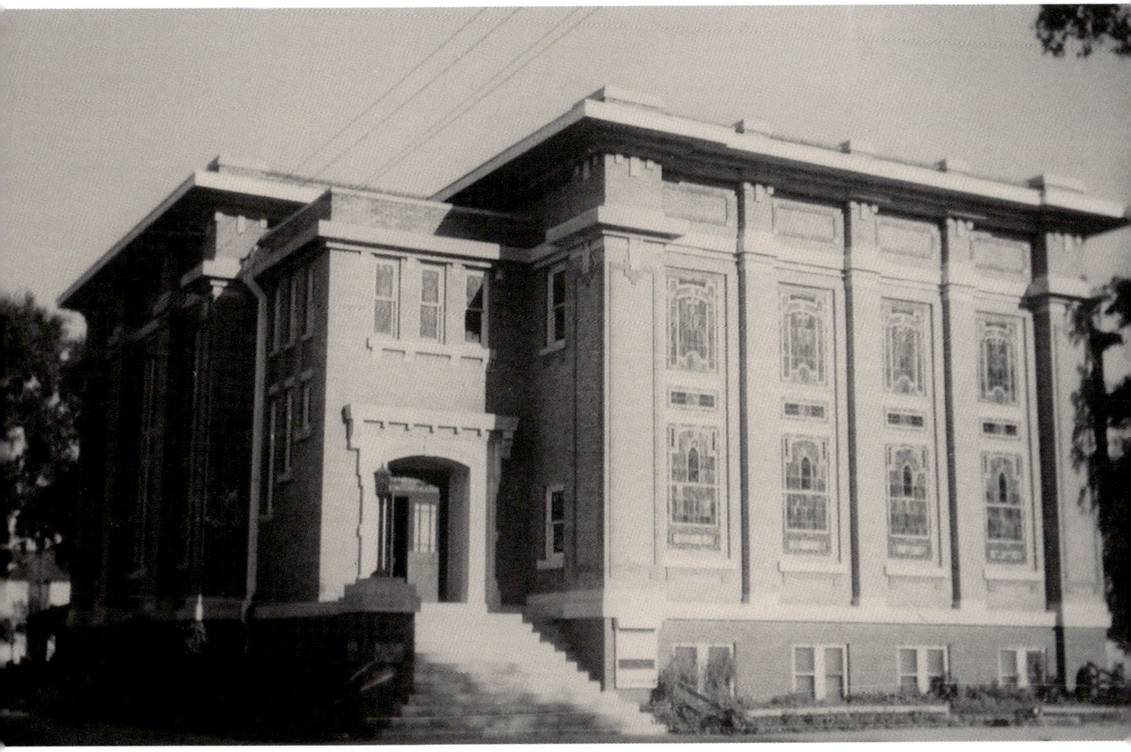

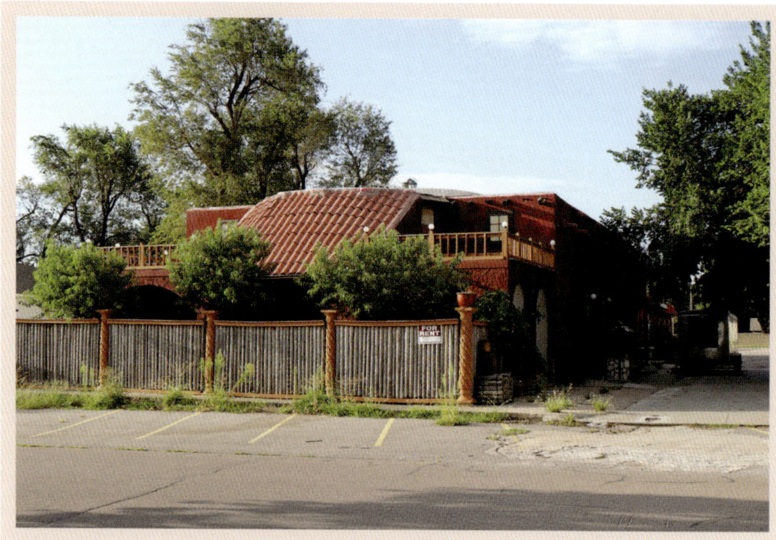

The Hillcrest Church of Christ was built in the middle of the block between Hillcrest Drive and Seventeenth Street along Texas Avenue sometime in the mid-1950s. The church was active until sometime in the early 1980s. The past photograph was taken in 1957; note that Texas Avenue was unpaved. In recent years, the building served as restaurants but currently is unused. Members of the Church of Christ in Woodward meet in a new building on Hanks Trail.

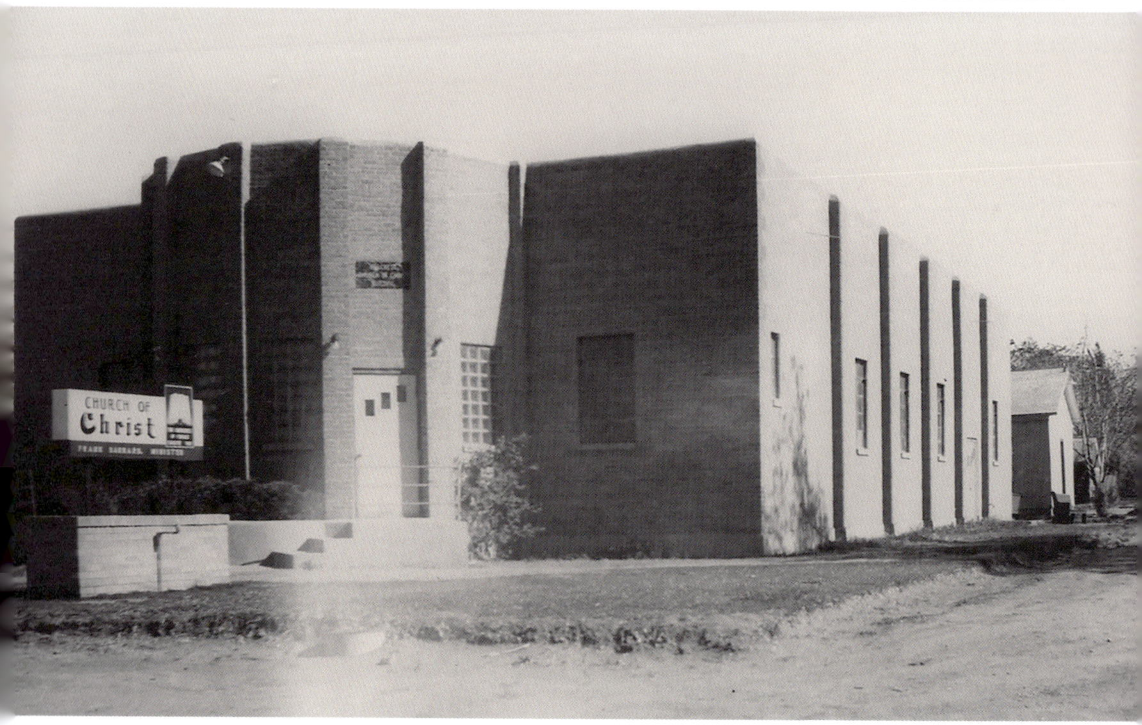

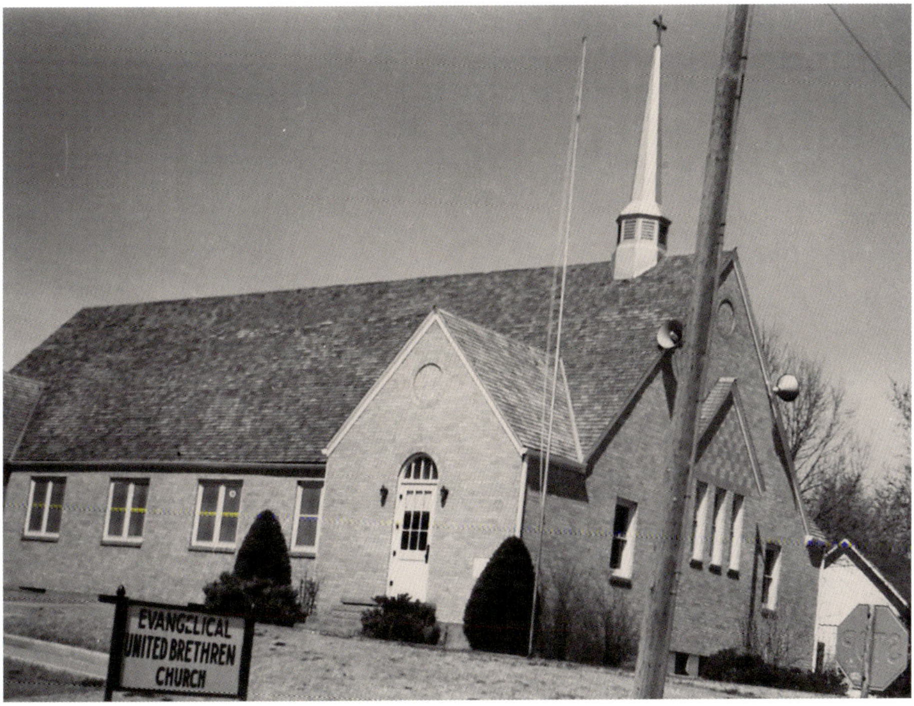

The original Evangelical United Brethren Church at Fourteenth Street and Texas Avenue was completely destroyed in the 1947 tornado. The new building, as seen above in 1957, was built soon thereafter. The union of Evangelical United Brethren churches and Methodist churches into the United Methodist Church took place in 1968. The congregation soon chose the name Faith United Methodist Church, and it has served its congregations ever since.

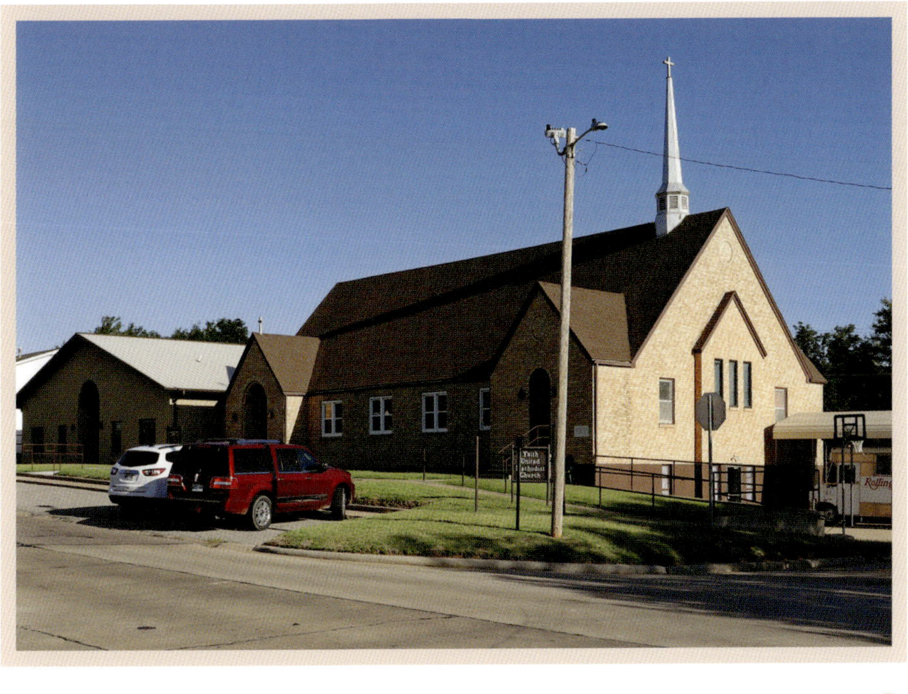

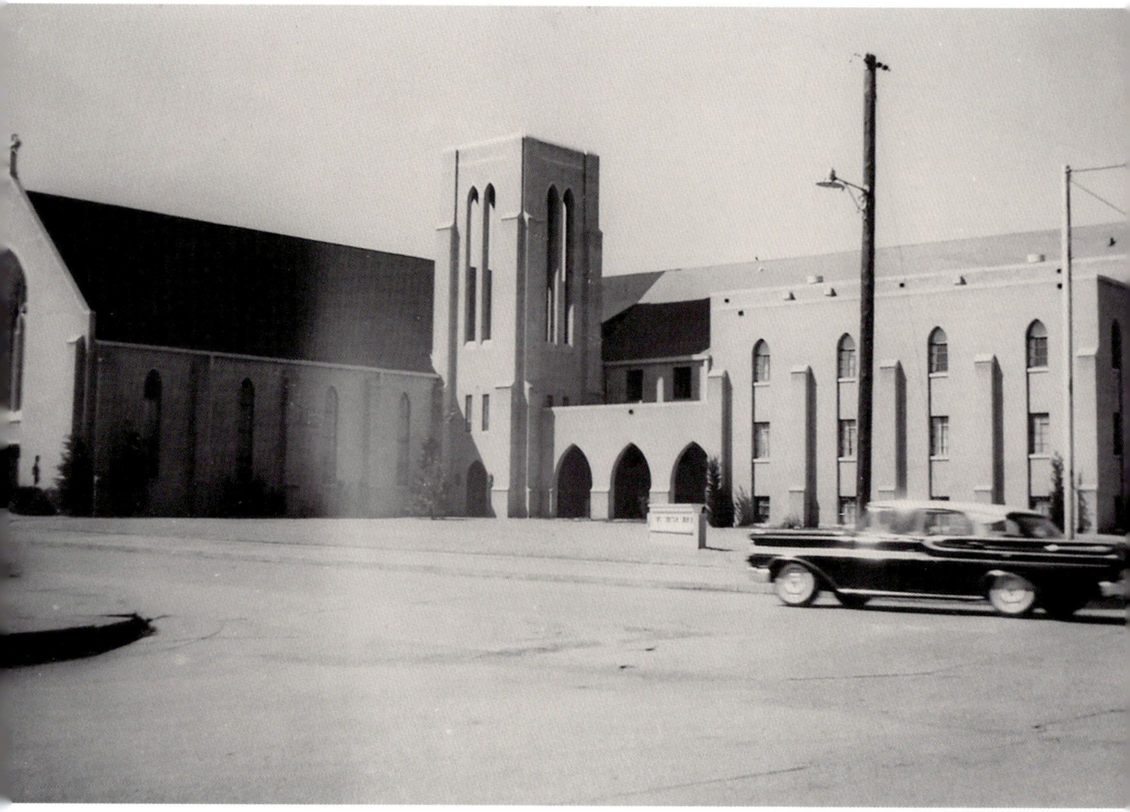

The First Christian Church was first organized in Woodward in 1902. The present building, with its impressive architecture on the southwest corner of Eighth Street and Oklahoma Avenue, was dedicated in 1952. Its cost of $75,000 had been paid in full. There was a mortgage burning ceremony in September 1962 to commemorate the church's 60th anniversary. The photograph below dates to the early 1960s and shows Oklahoma Avenue paved. (Above, courtesy of First Christian Church.)

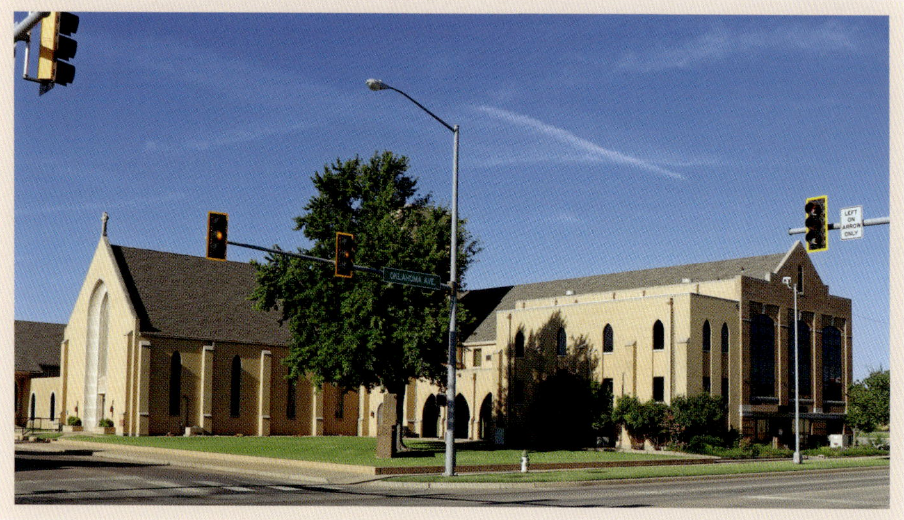

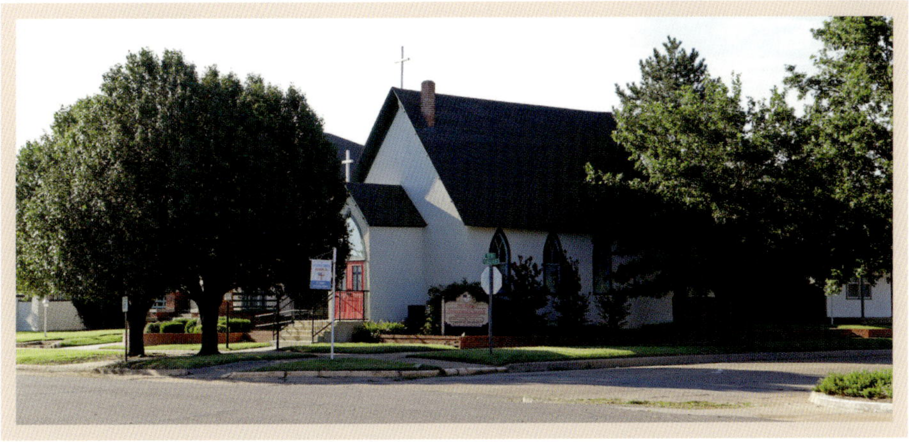

The story of St. John's Episcopal Church takes on near-legend status. For years, the story has persisted that the structure was on the US Army post of Fort Supply. The church was constructed on the corner of Seventh and Main Streets in 1893, making it the oldest still-standing church in Woodward. Parishioners built the church with whatever materials they had on hand. The church moved to its present location at Tenth Street and Texas Avenue in 1901.

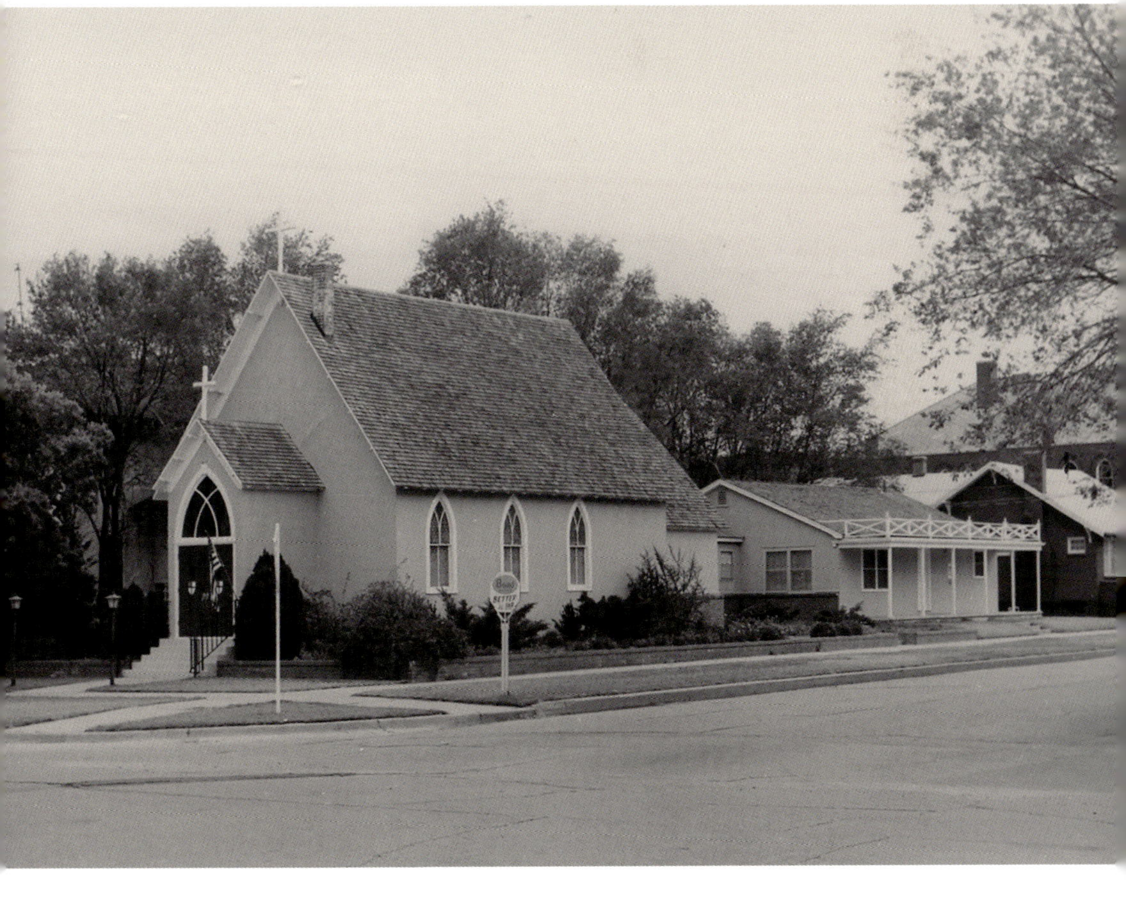

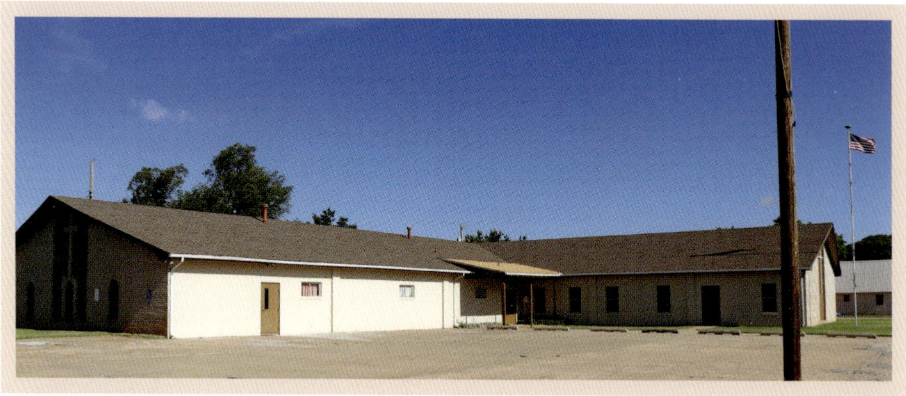

Elm Street Baptist Church has been serving its congregation from the corner of First Street and Elm Avenue since about 1974 as a mission of First Baptist Church. A major addition was made in 1976. Elm Street Baptist Church is affiliated with the Southern Baptist Convention, the largest Protestant denomination in the United States.

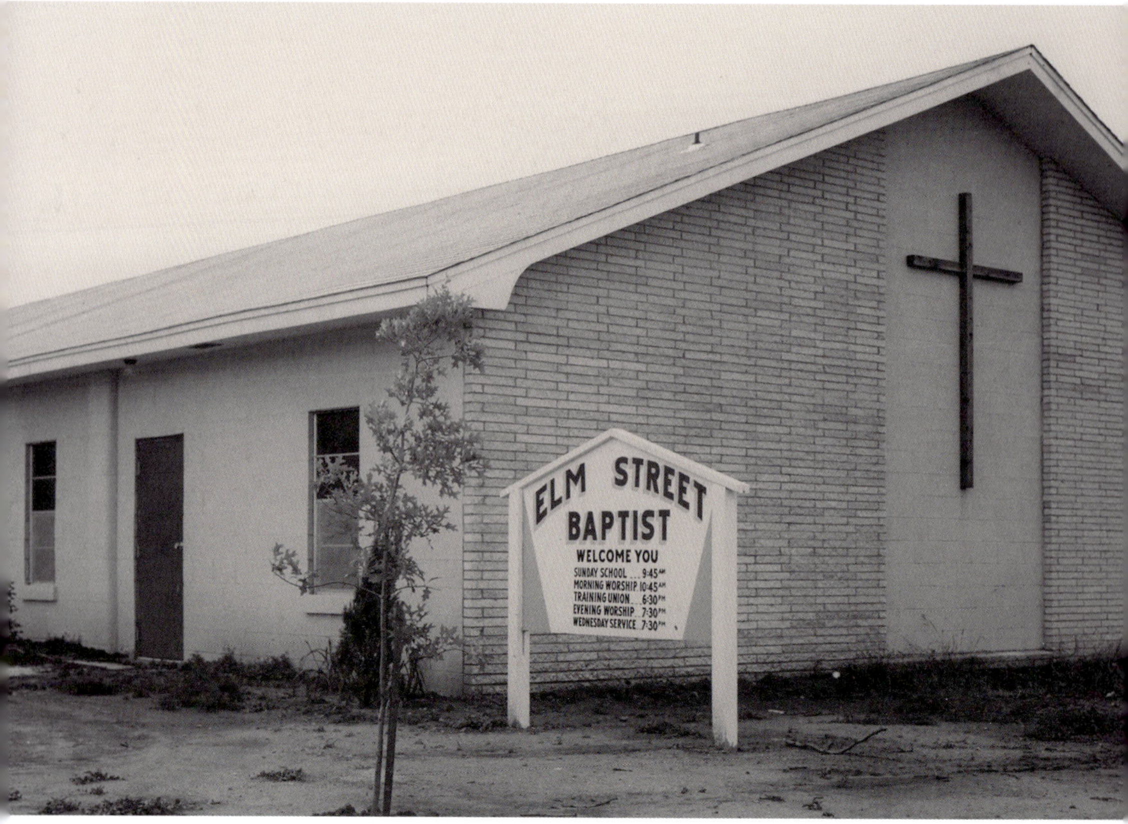

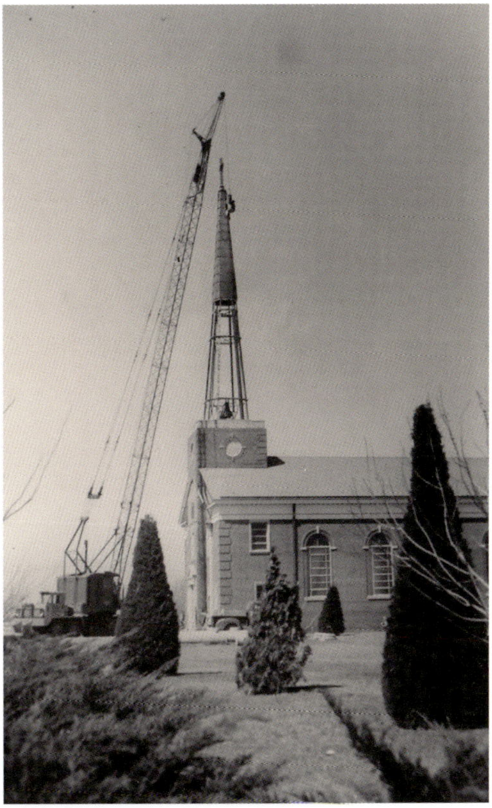

The original Saint Peter Catholic Church, constructed on the corner of Thirteenth and Main Streets, was destroyed in the tornado of 1947. Nothing was left standing but the entryway. Parishioners soon began celebrating Mass at the First Presbyterian Church until a Quonset hut was constructed at Twentieth Street and Texas Avenue. Construction on the new church began in 1952 and was completed in the fall of 1960. (Right, courtesy of Saint Peter Catholic Church.)

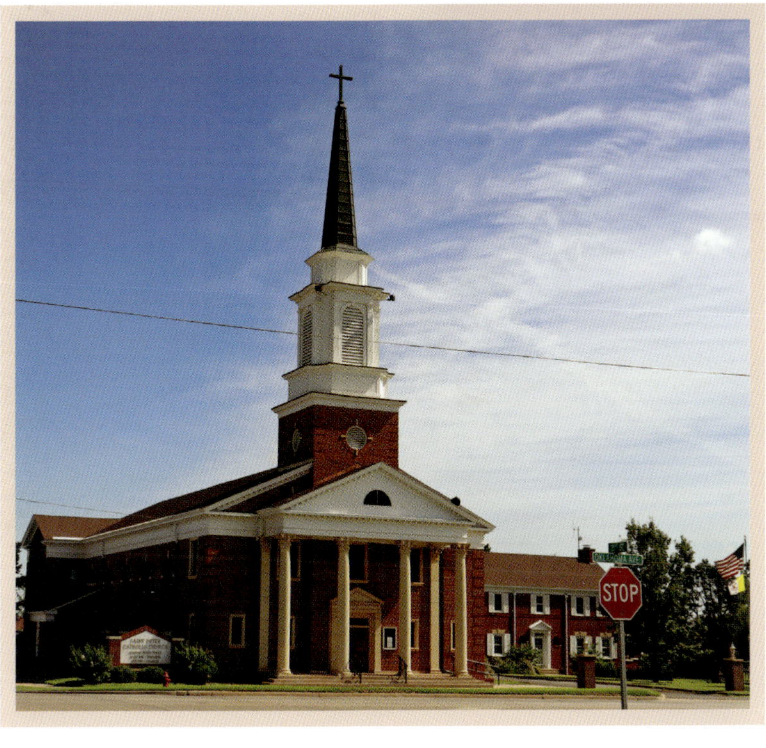

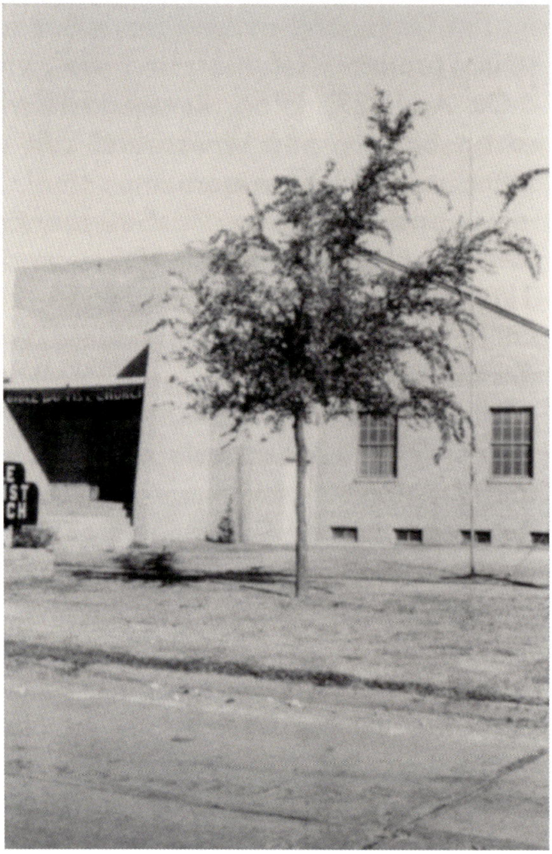

It could be said that Bible Baptist Church was the little church with big ambitions. An independent Baptist church, Bible Baptist's church has stood on the corner of Oklahoma Avenue and Seventeenth Street since October 4, 1959. The site was purchased with a loan from one of its members. The congregation had $151 in its building fund when it started but persevered, with members donating labor and materials until the structure was finished.

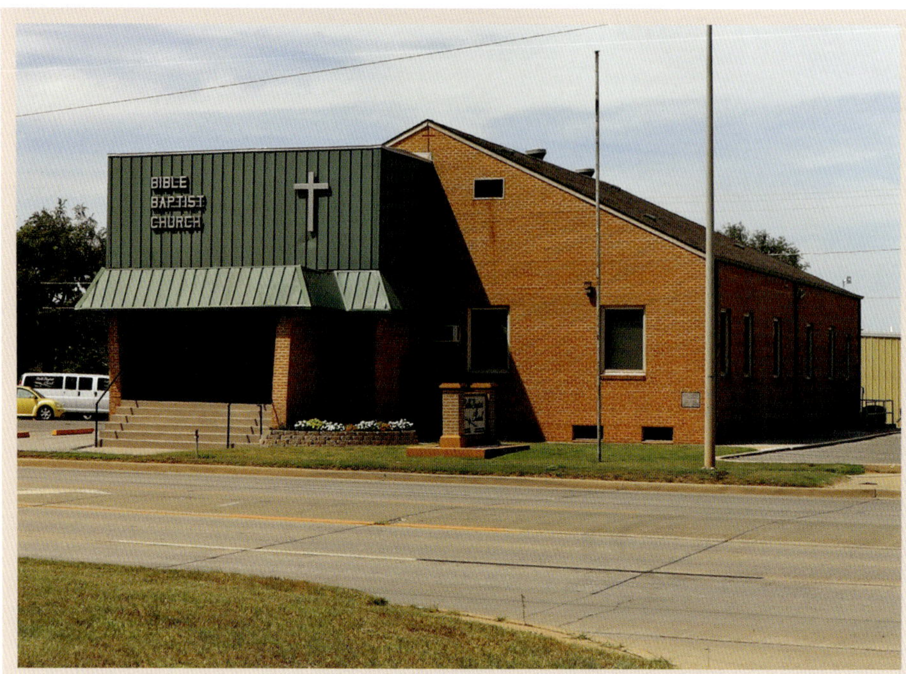

CHAPTER 5

EDUCATION

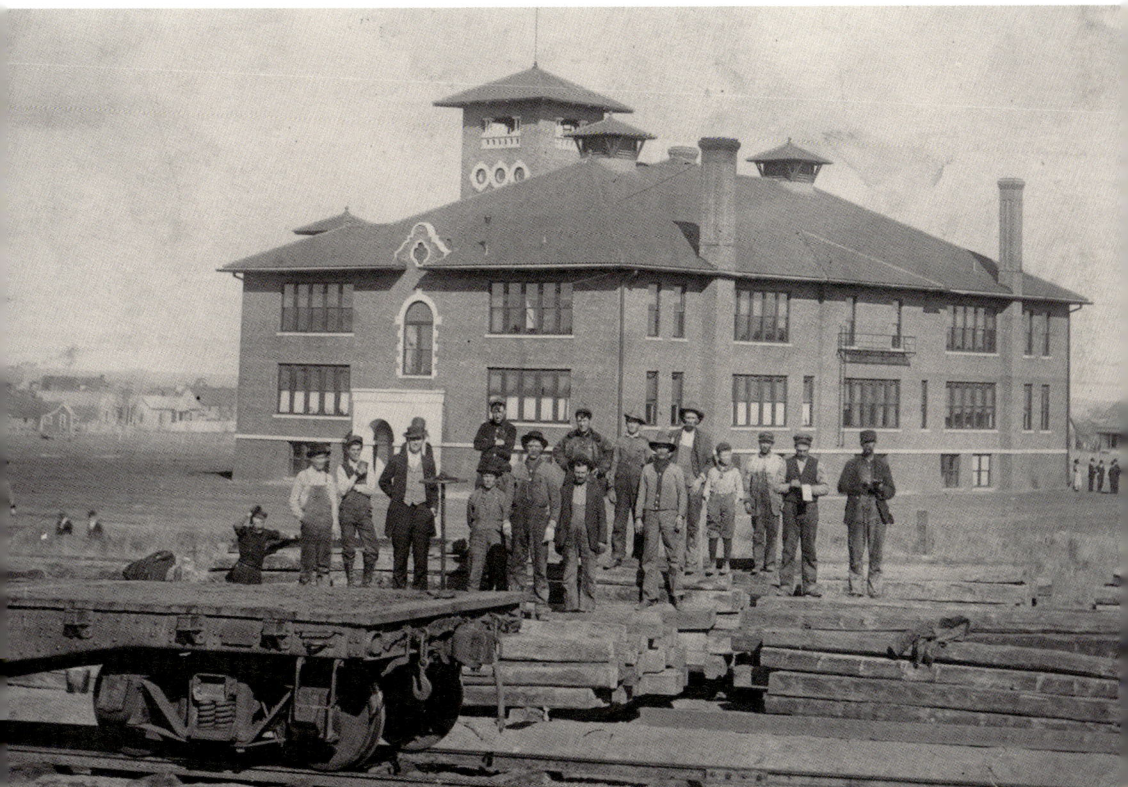

This photograph shows a work crew on the Missouri-Kansas-Texas Railway (also known as the Katy). In the background stands "Old Central," the high school built along Oak Avenue in 1910. Note the formally dressed man and little girl on the left.

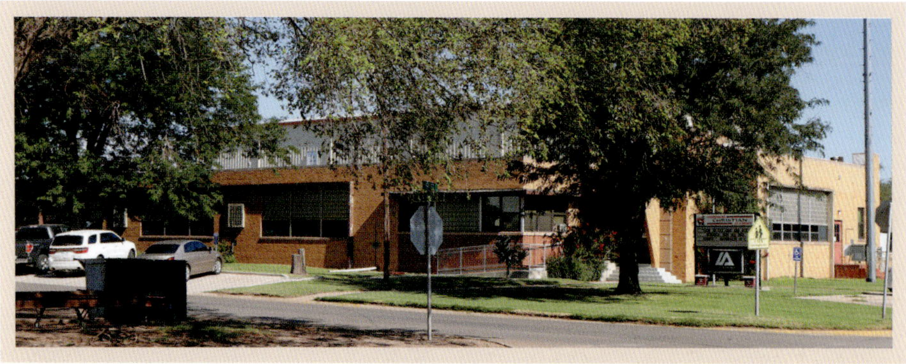

The present Westwood Elementary was rebuilt on the corner of Kansas Avenue and Nineteenth Street in 1947 after the original structure was destroyed in the tornado. Following the contraction of grade school buildings by Woodward Public Schools, the building became the Woodward Christian Academy in 1982, offering private school for children from age three through 12th grade.

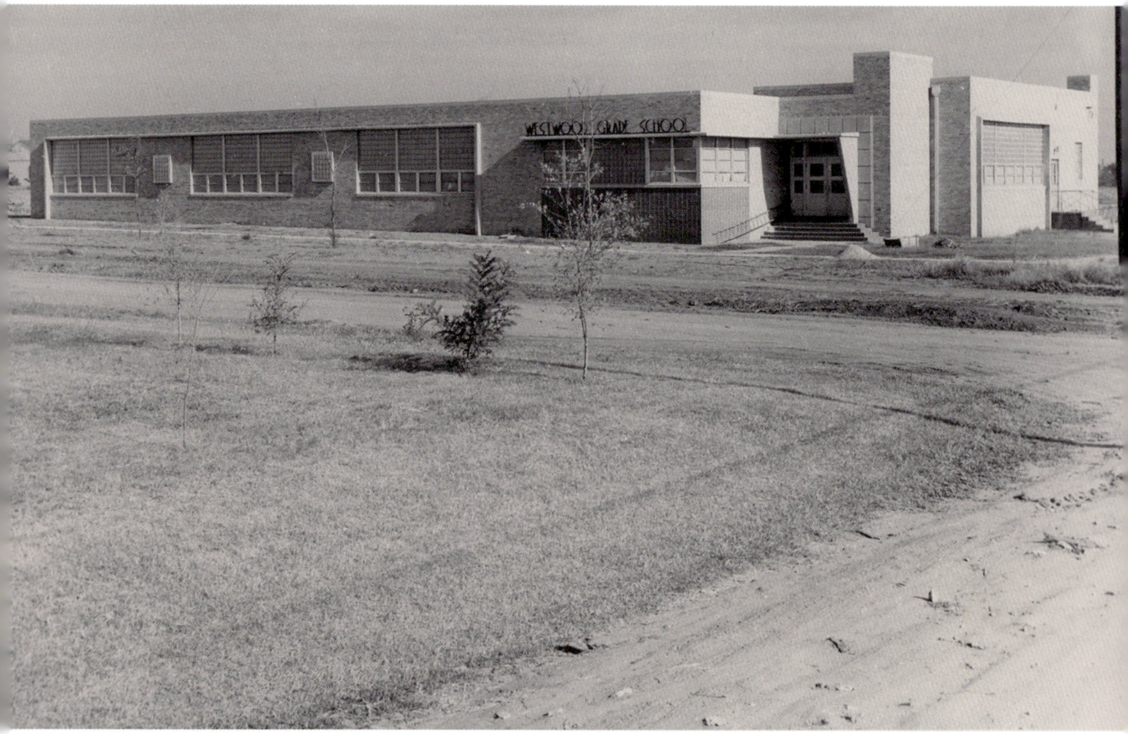

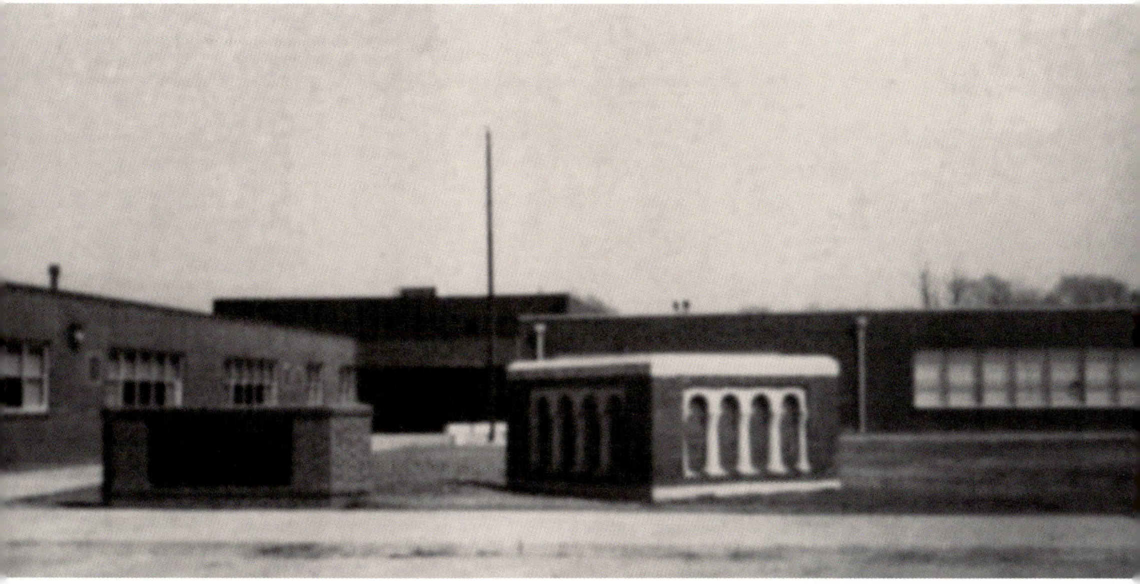

Named for the father of universal public education, Horace Mann Elementary has welcomed thousands of young minds through its doors since it was constructed around 1910, facing Second Street between Cherry Avenue to the south and Locust Avenue on the north. Originally known as East Ward School, it suffered comparatively minor structural damage during the 1947 tornado when two walls were knocked out of alignment. Today, the school teaches students in first through fourth grades. (Above, courtesy of Woodward Public Schools.)

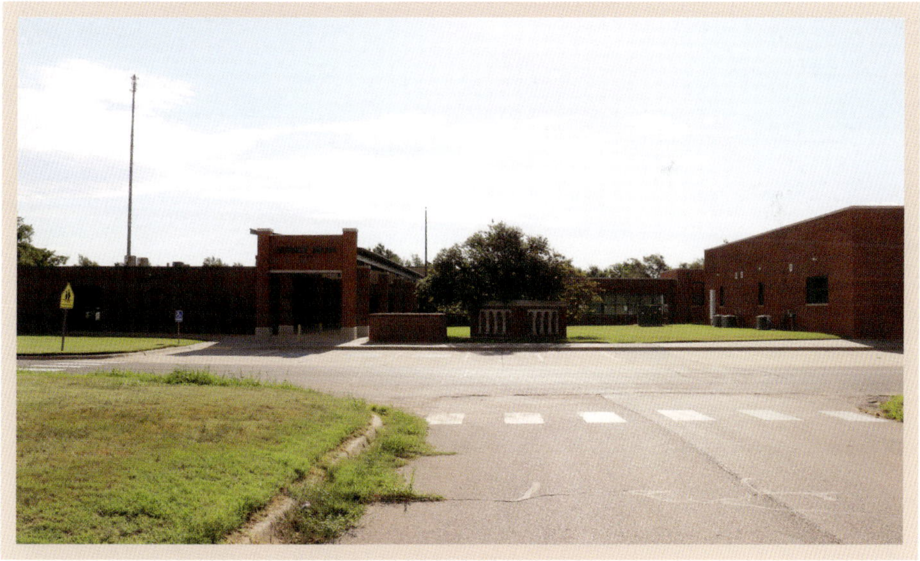

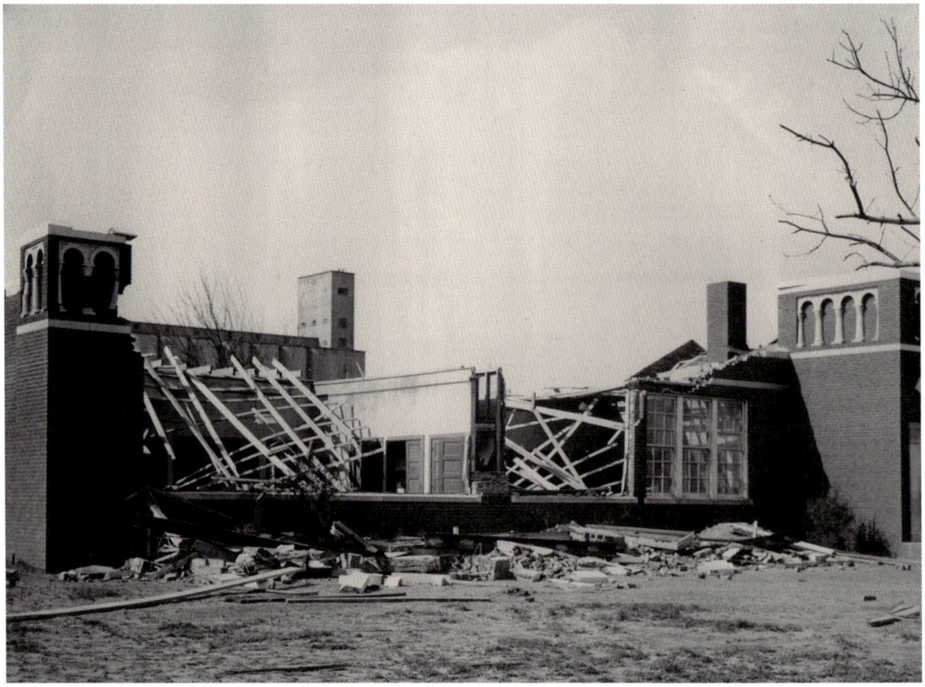

Madison Park Elementary, originally known as the North Ward School, was built facing Madison Avenue between Eighth and Ninth Streets in the early 20th century as a white frame building. During the late 1930s, a brick structure replaced the original building. It suffered extensive damage during the 1947 tornado. Madison Park was one of the schools that were closed in the early 1980s. It is now a Head Start school.

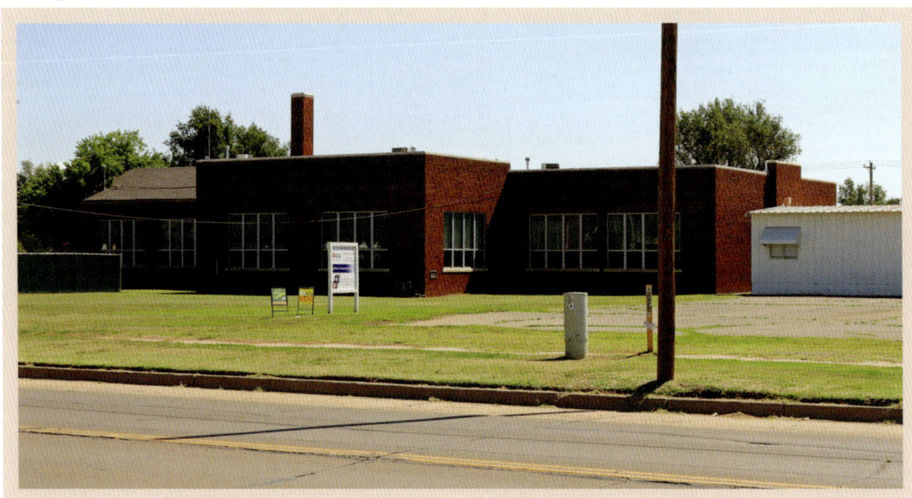

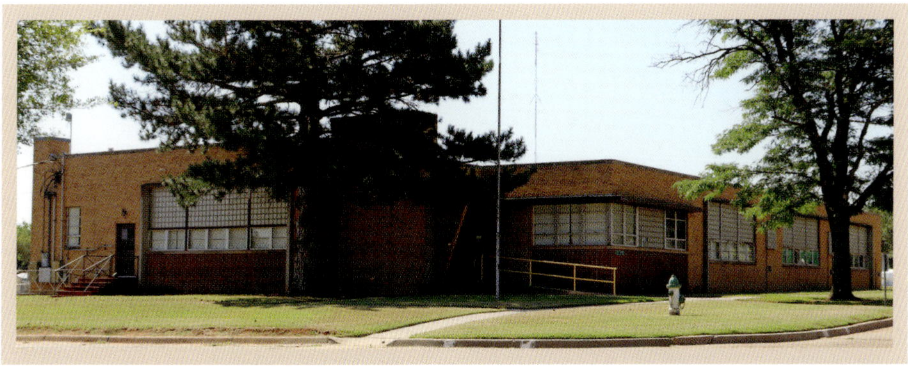

The time of Oak Park Elementary School as a grade school in the Woodward Public School System ended in the early 1980s when a reduction in student population necessitated the closing and consolidation of three elementary schools. The building currently serves two purposes, with the north end used for alternative education, and the Boomer Kids Club and Childcare Center on the south end.

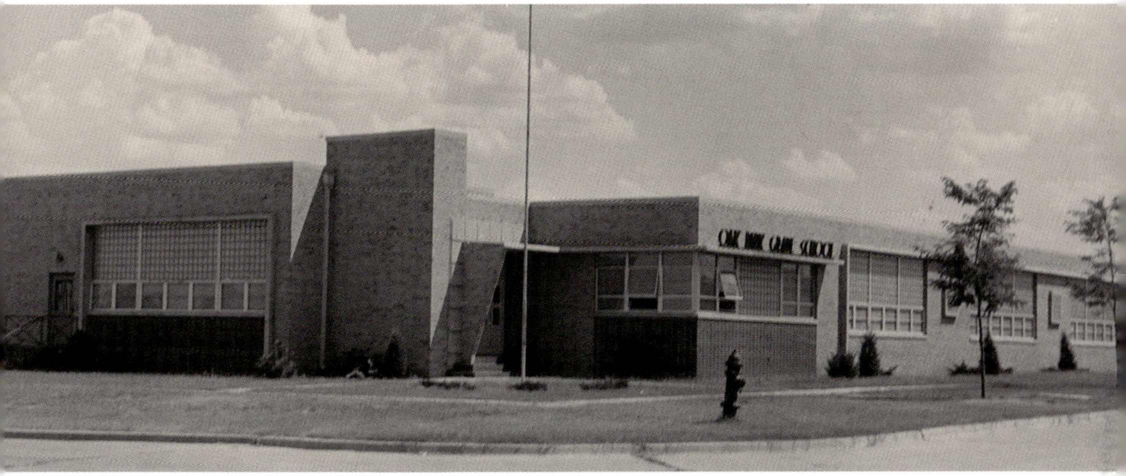

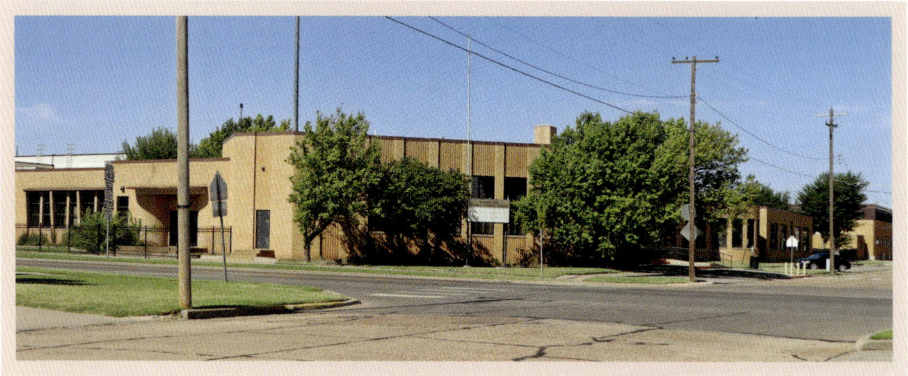

The building that housed Woodward Junior High School was built in 1948 just to the north of the old Woodward High School building at the corner of Ninth Street and Maple Avenue. It was part of a sprawling two-block campus that comprised the junior and senior high schools, two gymnasiums, a football field, a band building, and an industrial arts building. It became a fifth- and sixth-grade center in the early 1980s and is now part of Woodward Middle School.

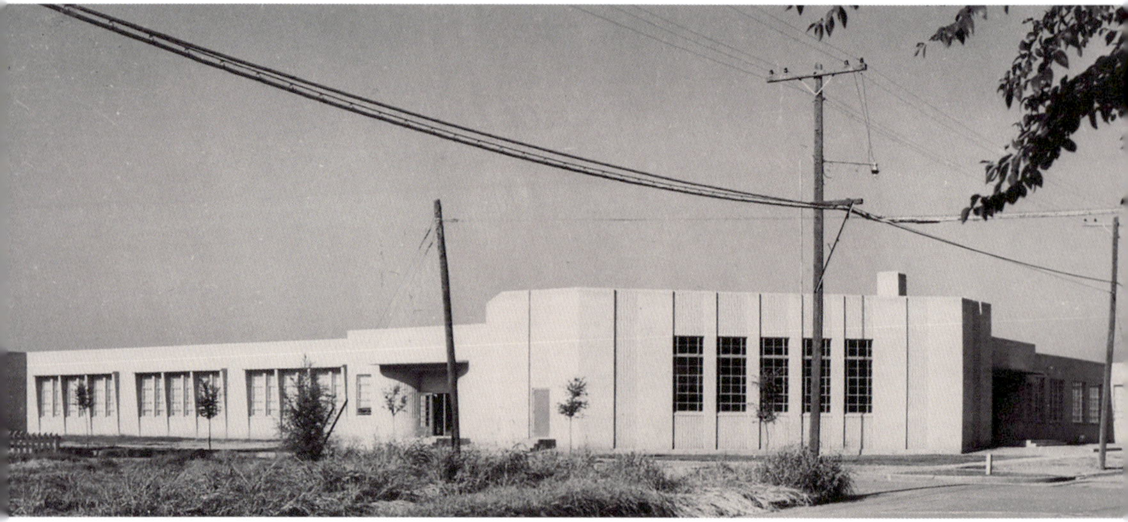

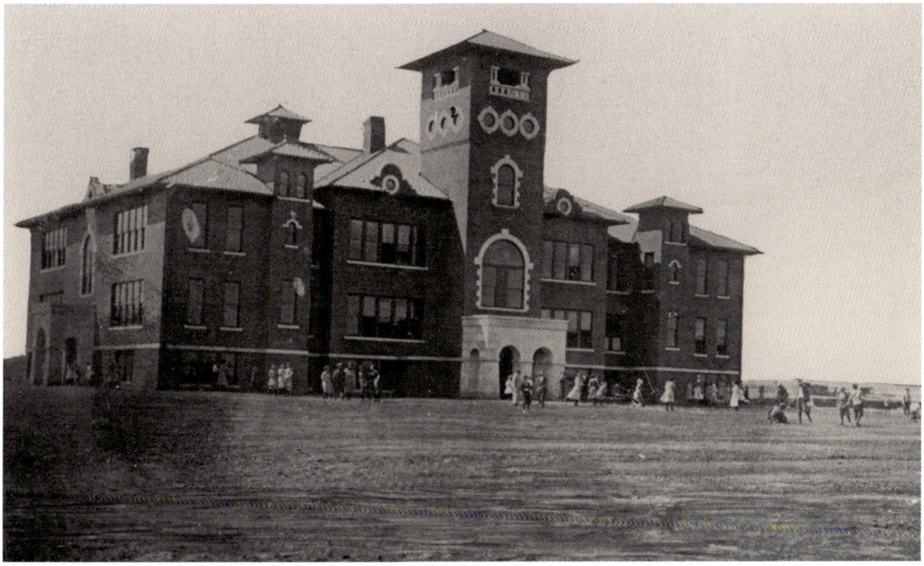

The building that was originally a high school for Woodward students was completed in 1911. After a new high school was built just to the east, some grade school and all junior high classes were moved to this building, which had become known as "Old Central." The tornado of 1947 wreaked havoc on the public school system. Old Central was damaged beyond repair and razed, spurring the construction of Woodward Junior High School.

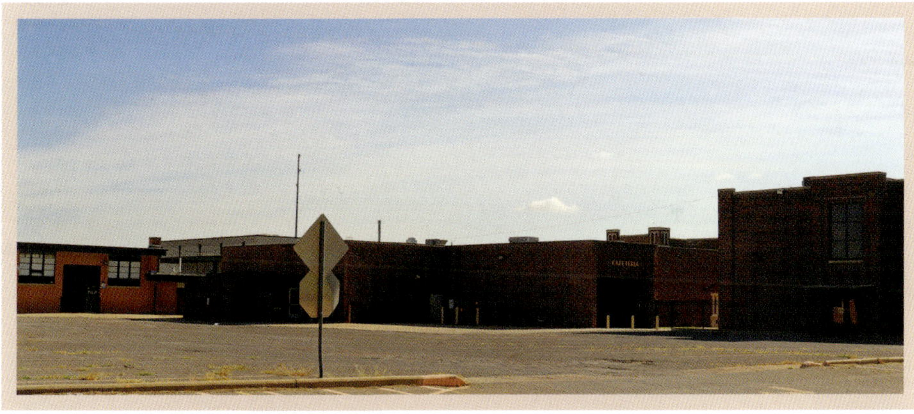

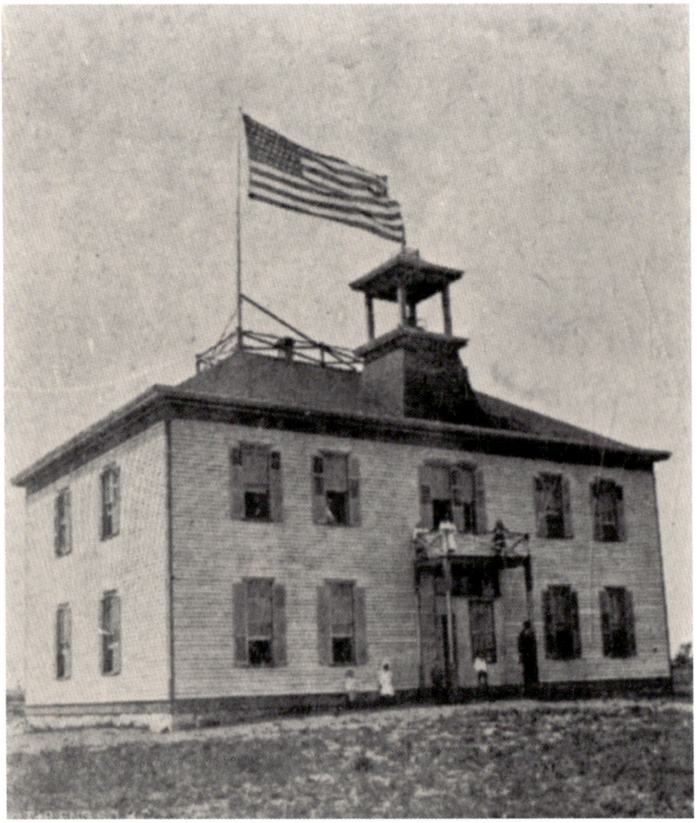

Referred to by the misnomer "Original School," the two-story structure built in the late 1890s was actually Woodward's second school, the first being a four-room building on the corner of Fifth and Main Streets that shared the lot with a saloon. That school burned down. The two-story school was built on the block that is today Centennial Park. Grade-school children were on the first floor, with high school students on the second floor. It burned down in 1910. (One cannot help but notice a pattern.)

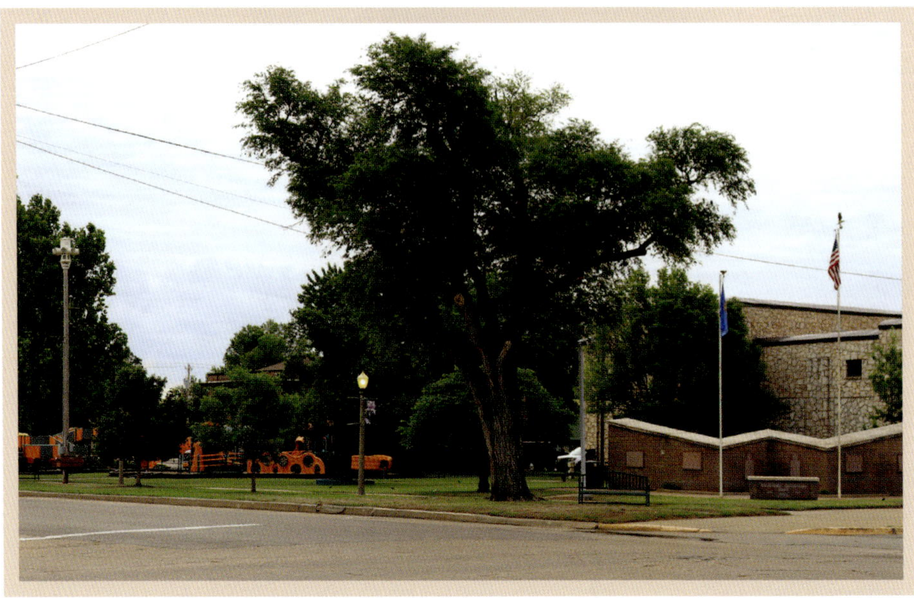

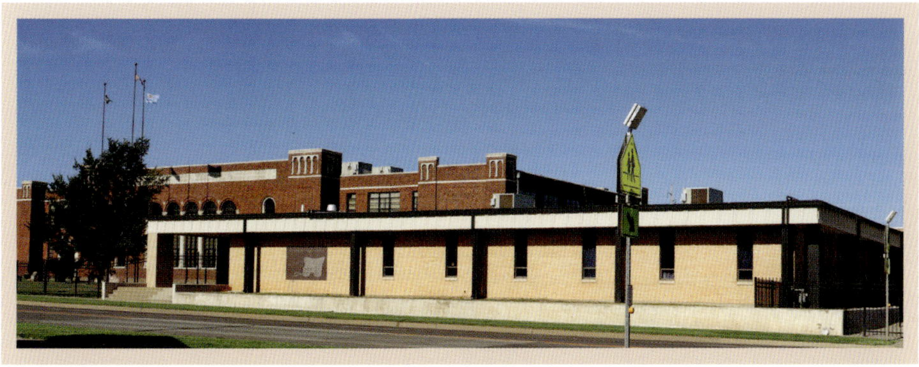

The building that served as Woodward High School for 49 years was constructed in 1929 along Ninth Street. It too suffered some damage in the April 1947 tornado but was repaired and opened for the school term starting in the fall of 1947. The building graduated thousands of students who went on to college or careers until 1978 when a new Woodward High School was built along Thirteenth Street near Downs Avenue. The building today is part of Woodward Middle School.

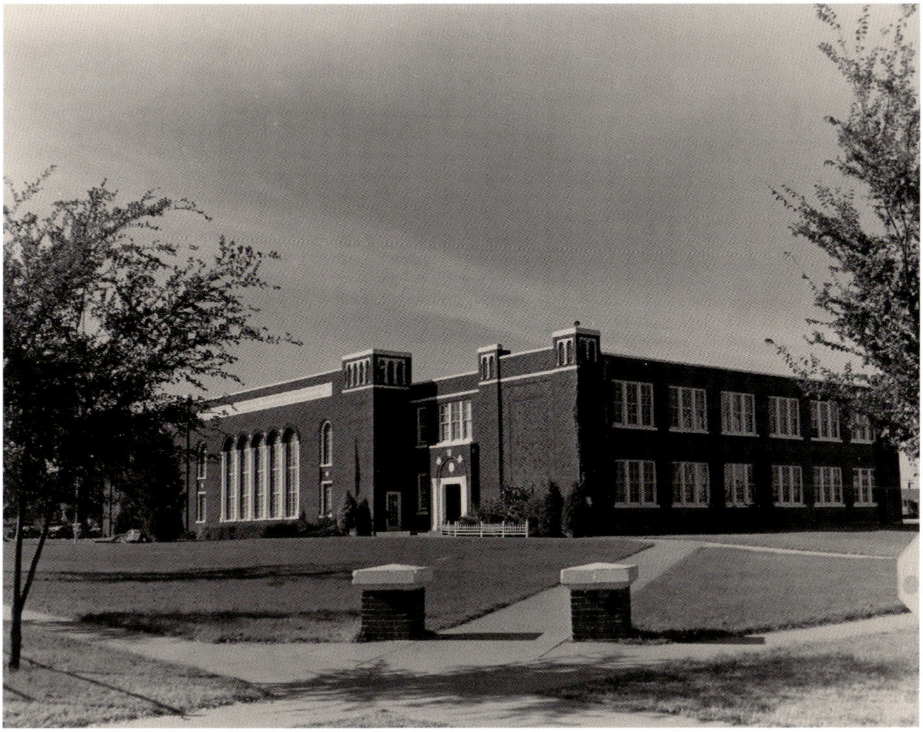

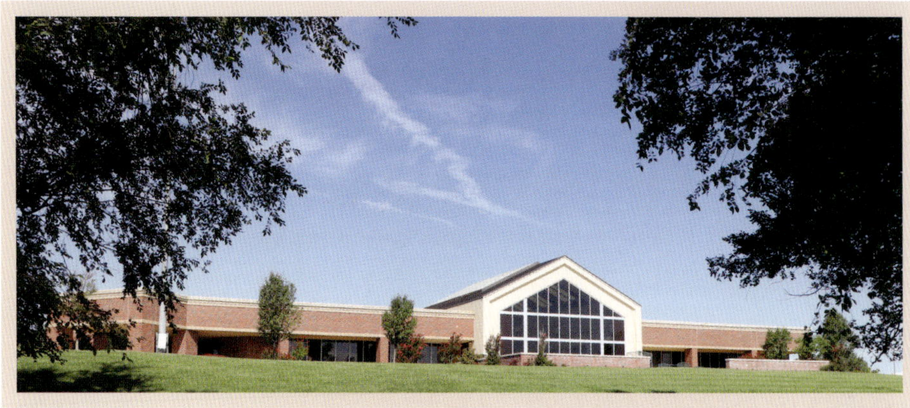

Built in 2002 to serve the higher education needs of Northwest Oklahoma, the Woodward campus of Northwestern Oklahoma State University is in a beautiful setting on a ridge overlooking a lake. The university offers a number of on-site undergraduate and graduate programs as well as distance learning. The photograph below shows the front of the building during construction. (Below, courtesy of Deena Fisher.)

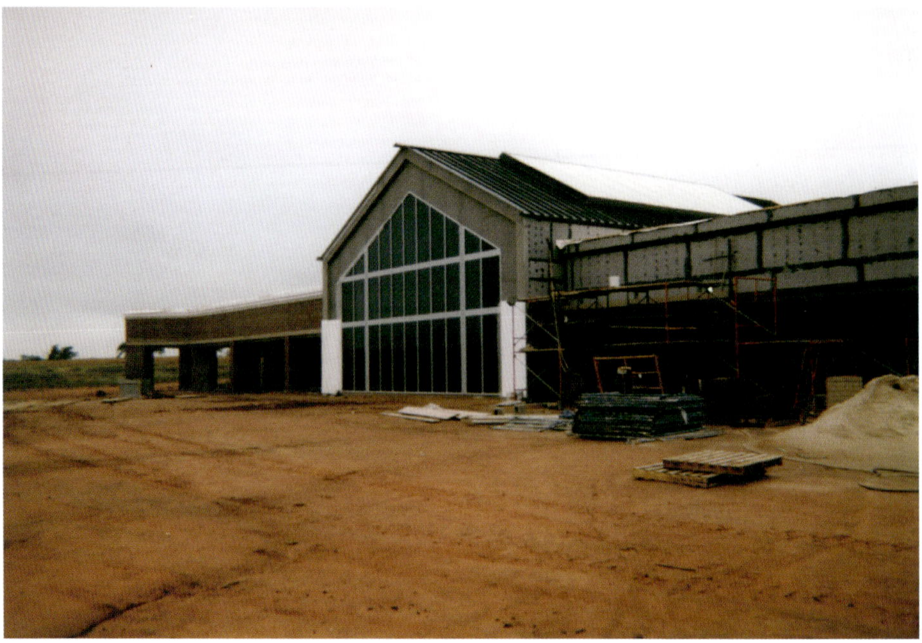

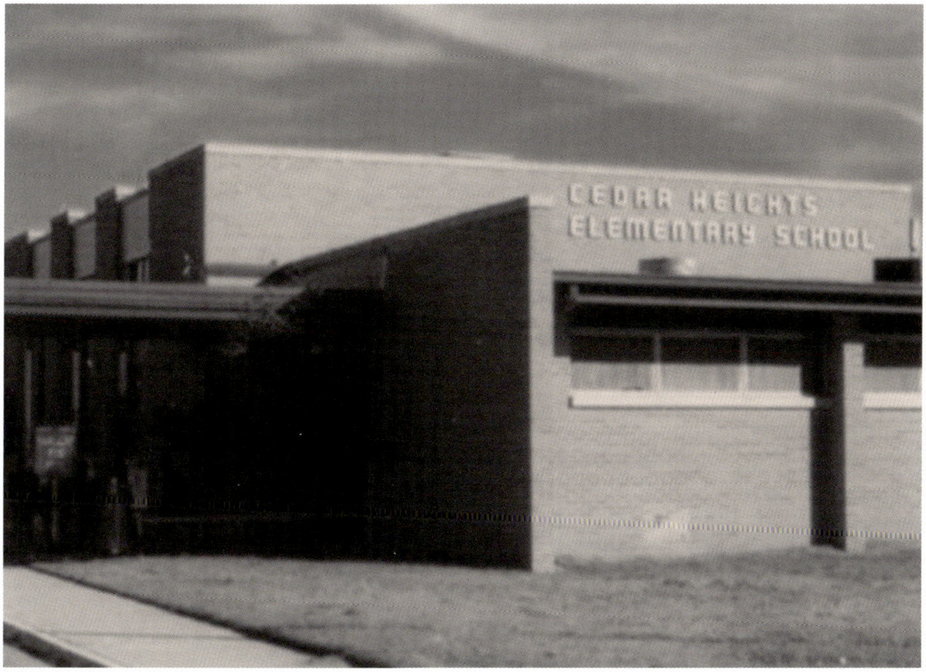

Cedar Heights Elementary School opened in the fall of 1961 at the intersection of Twenty-Second Street and Cedar Avenue. The addition of the school adjacent to the field station at the time gave Woodward Public Schools a total of five elementary schools with 38 classrooms. As with the other elementary schools in the Woodward system, Cedar Heights offers first through fourth grades. (Above, courtesy of Woodward Public Schools.)

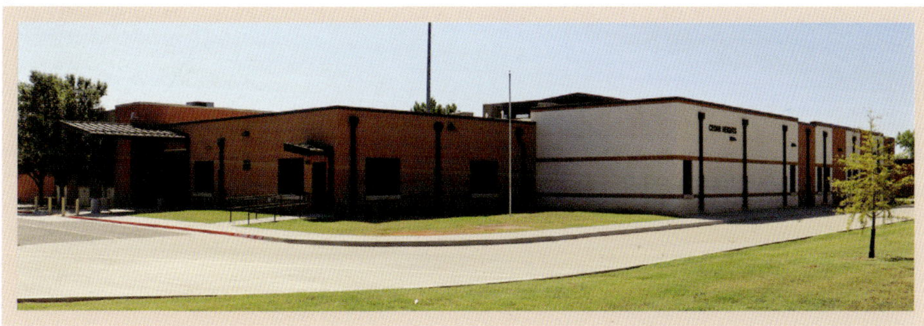

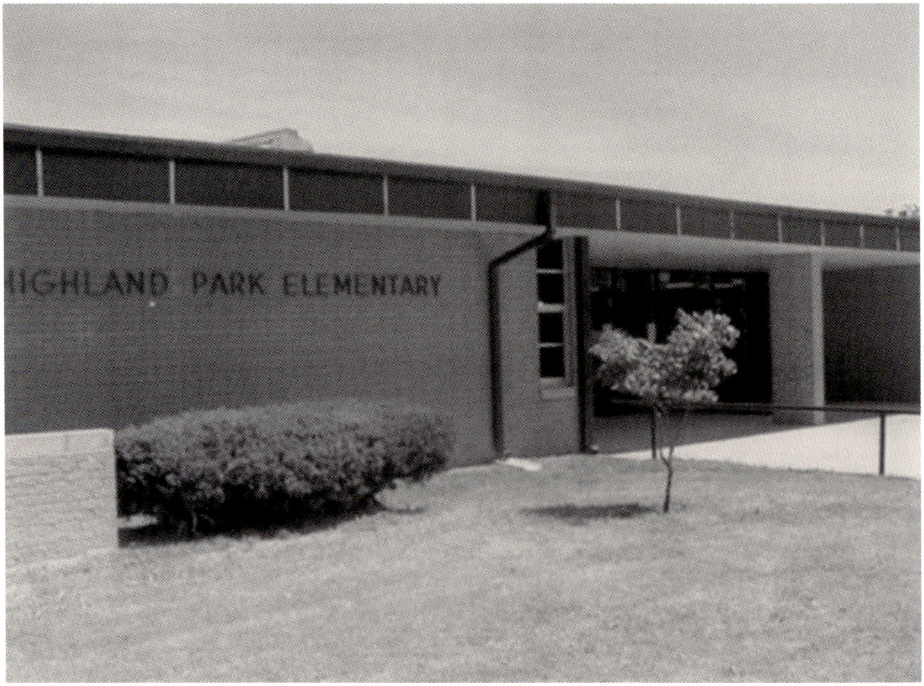

Construction of Highland Park Elementary, on the corner of Twenty-Eighth Street and Webster Avenue, commenced in 1968, and the school opened in the fall of 1969 to meet the needs of an expanding student population that followed the growth of housing additions on the west side of Woodward. Highland Park has an enrollment of approximately 255 students and ranks in the top 20 percent of Oklahoma public schools. (Above, courtesy of Woodward Public Schools.)

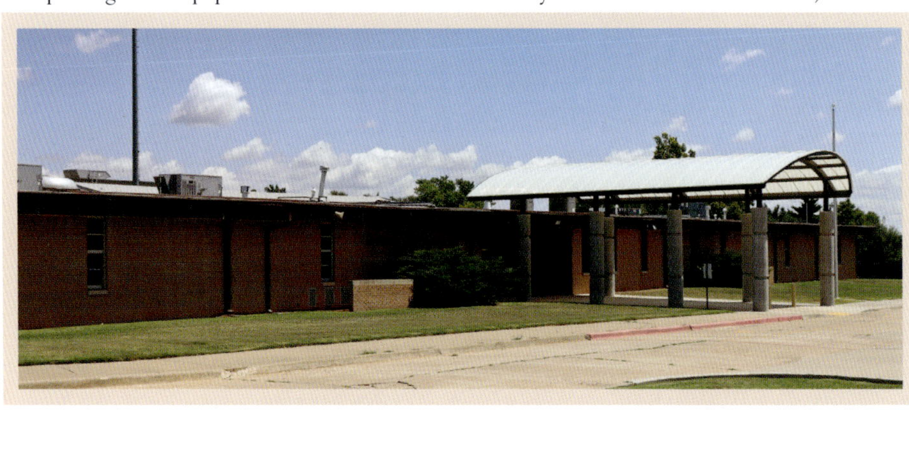

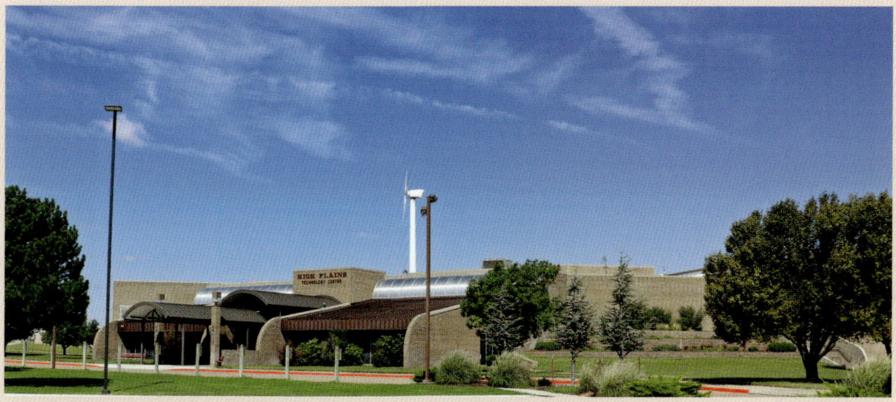

Classes at High Plains Area Vocational-Technical School for nursing students began in 1982. By August 1984, the building at the corner of Thirty-Fourth Street and Hanks Trail was completed, and other classes began. The school offers courses in business, industry training, and adult career development. In the fall of 2001, the official name for the school was changed to High Plains Technology Center. (Below, courtesy of High Plains Technology Center.)

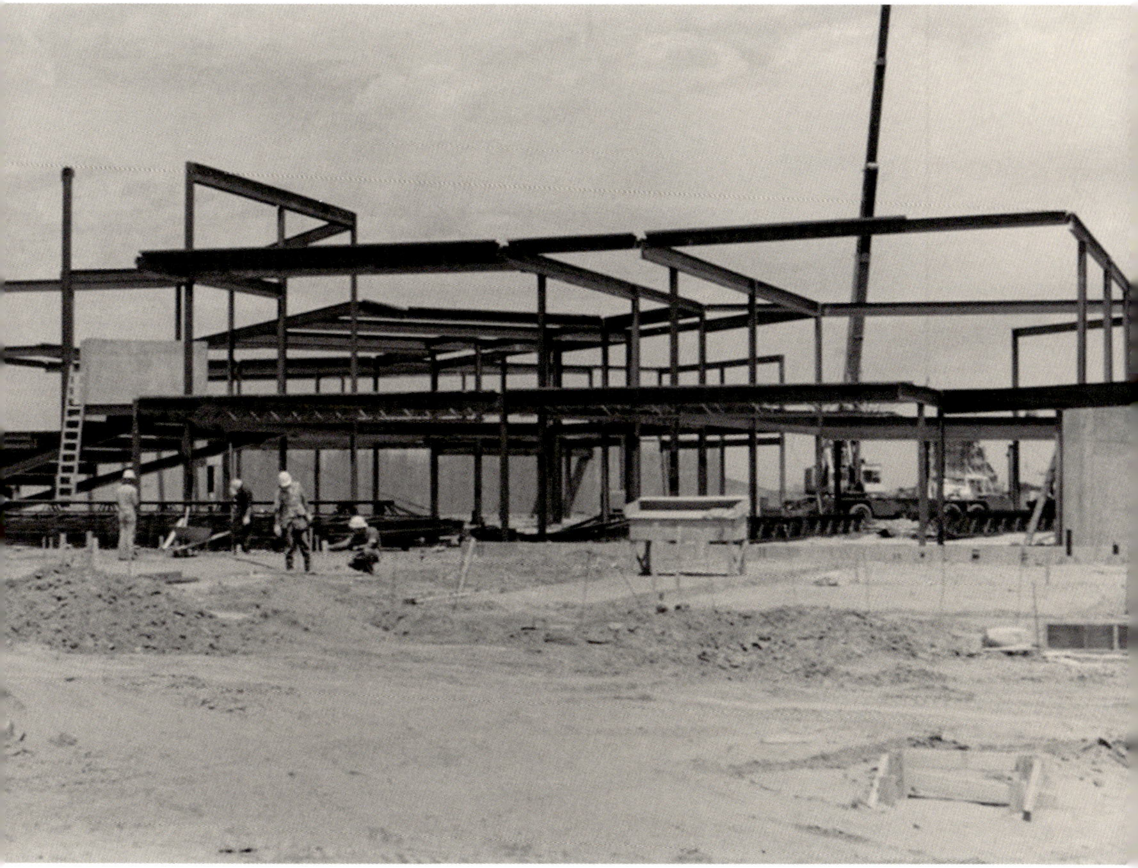